READ

Book Your Chair Solid
150+ Tips
To Grow Your Business

For Stylists, Salon Owners, Booth Renters,
Barbershops and Spas

Jeff Grissler and Eric Ryant

Ready, Set, Go!

Book Your Chair Solid: 150+ Tips to Grow Your Business for Stylists, Salon Owners, Booth Renters, Barbershops and Spas

© 2016 Jeff Grissler and Eric Ryant. All Rights Reserved.

No part of this book may be reproduced in any form or by any means, electronic, mechanical, digital, photocopying, or recording, except for the inclusion in a review, without permission in writing from the publisher.

First edition.

ISBN: 978-0-9906717-2-5 (paperback)
ISBN: 978-0-9906717-3-2 (digital)

Published in the U.S. by Ready Set Go Publishing, LLC
2118 Deer Island Lane
Wilmington, NC 28405
readysetgobooks.com

Printed in the United States of America.

Edited by Andrea Barilla and Jason Frye.

Go to *www.readysetgopublishing.com* to purchase other *Ready, Set, Go!* books.

Books Published by Ready, Set, Go! Publishing

The Start-Up Guide for Opening, Remodeling & Running a Successful Beauty Salon

A Salon Owner's Guide to Wealth

The Salon Building Bible

The Modern Salon in Pictures

How to Make Big Money at Your Salon by Offering 5-Star Service

The Start-Up Guide for Opening, Remodeling & Running a Successful Barbershop

Barbershop Now!

Cosmetology School Graduate - 1 Business Lessons

Cosmetology School Graduate - 2 Life Lessons

Cosmetology School Graduate - 3 How to get a J.O.B. in a Salon

Salon & Booth Rental Employee Handbook

Book Your Chair Solid: 150+ Tips to Grow Your Business For Stylists, Salon Owners, Booth Renters, Barbershops and Spas

TABLE OF CONTENTS

Introduction   1
How This Book Will Help You Find Clients   2
How to Use This Book   2
Finding Clients Is a Lot Like Dating   3
    Part 1: Where to Find Clients   4
    Part 2: Attract Clients Like Bees to Honey   5
    Part 3: Get Ahead of Your Competition   6
    Part 4: Giving Back   6
Dating (Client-Winning) 101: How Winning Clients is a Lot Like the Dating Game   7
    First Impressions Count: Looks and Personality   7
    Dress for Success: The Looks Part   8
    Style versus Trends   9
    Have a Positive Attitude, and Know What You and Your Salon/Spa/Barbershop Has to Offer: The Personality Part   10
    You Have to Ask: Put Yourself Out There   11
    Are You Afraid You'll Have TOO MANY Clients?   14

PART 1: Where to Find Clients

Networking   17
Tip 1   Friends and Family: Aunt Sally and Uncle Hugh   20
Tip 2   The People You See at Work: And There Are Many More Than You Think   21
Tip 3   Past Jobs: *As Long as You Didn't Say "Goodbye Suckas!" When You Left*   24

Tip 4	Former Teachers: Let Them See the Fruits of Their Labors	25
Tip 5	Connect the Dots: Reaching the Winners	26
Tip 6	Places You Go to All the Time—The *Cheers* Principle: Where Everybody Knows Your Name	27
Tip 7	Your Regular Coffee Shop	28
Tip 8	The Bank: Don't Be Afraid of The Suits	29
Tip 9	Schools and Day Care	30
Tip 10	The Kiddos: Being a Parent Can Actually Pay You for Once—With Clients	31
Tip 11	Church: Still the Best-Dressed Day of the Week	32
Tip 12	Rethink the After-Work Routine—Put Down the Remote and Ice Cream	33
Tip 13	Doctors' and Dentists' Offices	34
Tip 14	Accept All Social Invites: Go to Things	35
Tip 15	Join the Chamber of Commerce . . . Don't be Afraid to Admit You Don't Know What it Is; Just Read On!	37
Tip 16	Join and Attend Business Networking Groups and Events	38
Tip 17	Join Anything! (Book Club, Shuffleboard, Skee-Ball Group, Knitting Group, Monday Night Poker Club—Whatever Floats Your Boat)	39
Tip 18	Your Day Is Full of Opportunities—or Are You Missing Them?	40

Form Partnerships   45

Tip 19	Big Names in the Community—Hook Up with These People!	50
Tip 20	Local Hotels That Don't Have a Salon or Spa	51
Tip 21	Tanning and Nail Salons (Partner with Them, or Start Offering These Services)	52
Tip 22	Gyms, Yoga, and Pilates Studios Attract Attractive People	53
Tip 23	Dance Studios and Dance Moms	54
Tip 24	Theaters and School Productions: Hair and Makeup Make the Show	55
Tip 25	Restaurants and Health Stores	57

Tip 26	Clothing Stores (Women's and Men's)	58
Tip 27	Realtors, Home Builders, Homeowner Associations, and Apartment Complexes: Reach the New People Before Anyone Else Does	59
Tip 28	Small Business Development Centers	61
Tip 29	Life and Business Coaches	62
Tip 30	Dermatologists (The Money-Makers)	63
Tip 31	Home Parties: Partner with Friends Who Sell Things	64

Fun Partnership Ideas

Tip 32	Collaborative Deals	65
Tip 33	Cross-Business Raffle	66
Tip 34	Co-sponsored Events and Seminars	67
Tip 35	Partner with a Wedding Planner	68
Tip 36	Partner with a Photographer	69
Tip 37	Partner with a Bridal Shop and Tux Rental	70
Tip 38	Partner with a Jeweler	71
Tip 39	Partner with Catering Companies, Bakeries, or Cake Designers	72
Tip 40	Partner with Wedding Venues	73
Tip 41	Partner with a Limo Company	74
Tip 42	Partner with a Florist	75

Fun Ideas for Wedding Partnerships

Tip 43	Sponsor a Free Wedding	76
Tip 44	The Wedding Industry	77

Trade Shows and Community Events   81

Tip 45	Wedding/Bridal Shows and Expos	86
Tip 46	Maternity/Baby Expos	87
Tip 47	Fashion Shows	88
Tip 48	Home and Garden Shows	89
Tip 49	Sponsor an Event	90

Tip 50	Other Fairs and Festivals	91
Tip 51	Beer Fests	92
Tip 52	Business Networking Events	93
Tip 53	Car and Boat Shows	94

PART 2: Attract Clients Like Bees to Honey

Social Media — 97

Tip 54	Create or Revamp Your Website	100
Tip 55	It's a MUST to Make Your Site Mobile-Friendly	103
Tip 56	Text-Message Marketing	104
Tip 57	Offer E-gifts	105
Tip 58	Facebook	106
Tip 59	Digital Lookbooks and Online Portfolios	110
Tip 60	Google+ and Google My Business	111
Tip 61	Twitter	113
Tip 62	Instructional Videos (YouTube, Vine, Instagram)	115
Tip 63	Start a Beauty or Grooming Blog	117
Tip 64	Digital/E-newsletters	118
Tip 65	Create How-To Stories on Snapchat & Periscope	119
Tip 66	Check-In Apps: Yelp Can Help	120
Tip 67	Groupon and LivingSocial: Daily Deal Sites	121
Tip 68	Craigslist Ads: Free Advertising!	123

Traditional Advertising — 124

Tip 69	Television Ads	125
Tip 70	Radio Spots	126
Tip 71	Newspaper Ads	128
Tip 72	Ads in Hometown Magazines	130
Tip 73	Coupon Mailings	132
Tip 74	The Yellow Pages	134
Tip 75	Distribution of Marketing Materials	135
Tip 76	Signage	136

Promotions and Special Events

Tip 77	Sweetening the Deal: Promotions and Special Events	138
Tip 78	Hire a Street Team	143
Tip 79	Fun Daily and Weekly Specials	145
Tip 80	Blackboard Special	147
Tip 81	Sale Days—LIMITED TIME ONLY!	148
Tip 82	Seasonal Events	149
Tip 83	Add Pumpkin to Your Menu: The Power of the Season	151
Tip 84	Holiday Promotions and Events	152
Tip 85	Christmas	153
Tip 86	Themed Promotions and Events	155
Tip 87	Movies, TV, and Books Tie-In Promotions and Events	156
Tip 88	Fun, Creative Package Deals	157
Tip 89	Roll Out a New Line of Products or Colors	158
Tip 90	Monthly Specials	159
Tip 91	Quickie Services	160
Tip 92	Frequent-Service Punch Cards	161
Tip 93	Customer-Referral Cards and Rewards	162
Tip 94	Friends-and-Family Certificates	163
Tip 95	Birthday Program	164
Tip 96	Celebrate Salon Anniversaries	165
Tip 97	Celebrate VIP Clients	166
Tip 98	Celebrate New Moms and Dads	167
Tip 99	Senior Discount	168
Tip 100	Catch New Residents First	169
Tip 101	Celebrate New Customers with a Welcome Package or Gift	171
Tip 102	Giveaways and Freebies	172
Tip 103	Tips for Slow Nights or Days	173
Tip 104	Makeover Mondays	174
Tip 105	Open on Sundays	175
Tip 106	Neighborhood Meet and Greet	176
Tip 107	Girls'-Night-Out Promotions and Events	177
Tip 108	Handbag Swap	178

Tip 109	Beard Events	179
Tip 110	Father/Son and Mother/Daughter Events	180
Tip 111	Military Discount	181
Tip 112	Night to Honor Those in Uniform	182
Tip 113	Wine Tasting or Craft Beer Night	183
Tip 114	Have a Fashion Show	184
Tip 115	Image Makeovers	186
Tip 116	Beauty/Grooming How-To's and Wellness Seminars	187
Tip 117	Artistic Director Contest	188
Tip 118	Celebrity Visit	189
Tip 119	Woo Back MIA Clients: The Gifts and Flowers	190

PART 3: Get Ahead of Your Competition

Be Business Savvy

Tip 120	Be Business Savvy—Good Business Practices Win and Maintain Clients	193
Tip 121	Build Your Business Skills	195
Tip 122	Keep Your Employees Happy	196
Tip 123	Capture Client Info	197
Tip 124	Handwritten Notes	198
Tip 125	Pay Attention to Your Competition	199
Tip 126	Merchandising	200
Tip 127	New Product Offerings	201
Tip 128	Add Another Service	202
Tip 129	Make Your Salon Male-Friendly	204
Tip 130	Become a Makeup Specialist	205
Tip 131	Make More Money from Your Current Clients: Suggest Additional or New Services	206
Tip 132	Brand Your Recipes	207
Tip 133	Location-Specific Services: Cater to Your Location and Its Clientele	208
Tip 134	Be the First in Town to Offer a Hot New Treatment or Technique	209

Tip 135	Offer Memberships for Guaranteed Income	210
Tip 136	Gifts with Purchase and Samples	211
Tip 137	Retail Boutique	212
Tip 138	Salon or Barbershop Décor	213
Tip 139	Get Out of the Salon	215

Out-of-the-Box Ideas

Tip 140	Think Outside the Box	216
Tip 141	Be Your Town's Beauty Expert	218
Tip 142	Colleges and Universities	219
Tip 143	Visit Construction Sites: Chase Down the Men	221
Tip 144	Reach Out to Accountants During Tax Season	222
Tip 145	Dogwalk Fashion Show	223
Tip 146	Parties	224
Tip 147	Halloween and Costume Services	225
Tip 148	Reenactment Groups	226

PART 4: Giving Back

Give Back and Show Support

Tip 149	Give Back and Show Support	228
Tip 150	Choose Your Charity	230
Tip 151	Join a Local Volunteer Organization	231
Tip 152	Host a Fundraiser	232
Tip 153	Customer Appreciation Days	233
Tip 154	Think Pink: Breast Cancer Awareness	234
Tip 155	Think Red: Heart Disease Awareness	235
Tip 156	Monthly Causes	236
Tip 157	Shelters and Recovery Programs	237
Tip 158	Give-Back Day	238
Tip 159	Be Welcoming to the LGBT—Lesbian/Gay/Bisexual/ Transgender Community	239
Tip 160	Student and Teacher Appreciation	240

Tip 161	Event Donations	241
Tip 162	Sponsor a Local Charity Event or Community Organization, or Form a Team	242
Tip 163	A Newsworthy Salon	243
Tip 164	Locks of Love	244
Tip 165	Pamper People Who Could Really Use It	245

Implementation Guide — **247**
Conclusion — **253**
Speed Dating with Celebrity Stylists — **257**

INTRODUCTION

"Be a salesperson, not just a hair person."
—Jeff Grissler

The minute you graduate school and pass your state boards, it's up to you to get clients in your chair. No matter what your job may be in the beauty and grooming industry, the most difficult part is creating your market and getting new customers.

Success is simple: you need to get people in your chair.

> **WHO IS THIS BOOK FOR?**
> - Salons/spas/barbershops that need more clients
> - Salons/spas/barbershops that are losing clients
> - New stylists, barbers, etc. who want to build their book of business
> - Anyone in the service industry
> - Anyone wanting to grow his or her business

Every business has the same goal: to grow their customer base. Each may follow a different path to get there, but you all have the same intentions: personal development, growth, living life on your own terms, and, of course, financial independence.

When you signed up for cosmetology school, you knew you were creative enough to be successful in the field, but what you didn't realize was that being successful in the service business means wearing many hats. These hats come in various styles and sizes and can include salesperson, fashion consultant, public relations guru, marketer, social media expert, strategist, speaker, accountant, retailer, referee, boss—all while trying to juggle friends, family, and personal life.

Ultimately, having a strong client book is a matter of both attracting new clients and keeping those clients coming back after their first visit. The goal is a steady stream of customers customers day in and day out.

How This Book Will Help You Find Clients

We all need help sometimes. Sometimes, the idea well has run dry. Sometimes, the door isn't swinging open, and the silence rings in our ears. Sometimes, the appointment book is empty. Sometimes, we're worried whether we can keep the bills paid another month.

All these things can make us lose our confidence or even reconsider whether we picked the right job or the right field. How do we change things? What can you do to attract new business? How do you get clients back in your chair and grow your customer base?

We're here to help. This book contains 164 ideas designed to get your mojo back and fill your chair every hour of every day.

"The secret of getting ahead is getting started."
—Mark Twain

How to Use This Book

Now it's time to get started finding clients. We've made this book easy to reference by dividing it into four parts and several sections. Throughout you'll find our **Hammer Tips** and **Great Ideas**.

We've also included a ***Time and Money*** list that breaks down potential costs. You'll find them helpful when it comes to setting some of these plans in motion.

At the end of the book, we've included an ***Implementation Guide*** that will help you identify the kinds of things you need to consider when working with a more time-intensive idea, such as an event.

> **THIS BOOK IS FOR EVERYONE**
>
> You'll notice we use the term salon/spa/barbershop throughout the book and may sometimes just say salon for ease of reading. However, we believe the ideas in here are for anyone in the beauty business. Know we're referring to "you."

Finding Clients Is a Lot Like Dating

*"Let your hook be always cast.
In the pool where you least expect it, will be fish."*
—Ovid

You'll notice that while this book is packed full with tips on how to find clients and entice them to your salon/spa/barbershop, it's also packed with tips on how to win them once they *do* enter your salon. We're not looking for one-hit wonder clients here; we're looking for the staying power of The Rolling Stones, U2, and Fleetwood Mac.

We're looking for client commitment, not a one-night stand.

This book is about *getting* more clients, but it's also about *keeping* those clients. It's hard not to see the comparison to dating and marriage. You almost have to woo your clients with the goal of getting them to come back. But first, you need to *find some clients to woo*.

How do you find clients? *Where* do you find them?

Well, as you've heard it said, "You're not going to find anyone if you stay in every Friday night." Same with business. You need to get out there and pound the pavement.

PART 1: Where to Find Clients

1. Networking: This section will blow your mind because you will realize potential clients are everywhere. We'll highlight places to find clients you probably hadn't even thought of. This section is also full of additional tidbits such as why business cards still rule, top ten ways to rock a social event, how to use your local chamber of commerce, etc. We'll even address the fear of success—Are you afraid of getting too many clients and not being able to manage them?

2. Form Partnerships: Tons of businesses and individuals have clients who would be perfect for you as well. In the case of business, it's okay to have multiple partners and to share clients—we're not getting kinky here. We're talking in business. Consider businesses with similar client bases or businesses that are serving the client demographic you are trying to reach, and see if you can partner up with them. If we were going for a dating metaphor, this would be like asking your friends to set you up with their friends—in this case, you're wanting to *share clients*.

3. The Wedding Industry: Weddings are always going to be around, and brides and their wedding parties can be a huge client stream. Besides the dress, hair is the next most important thing. And makeup. And nails. This is the day girls want to look their most beautiful and guys their most handsome and suave. Yes, barbers and stylists, don't forget the men. So how do you find these brides? These grooms? This section will focus on partnering with other vendors in the wedding industry, maximizing your chances of reaching as many brides and grooms as you can.

4. Trade Shows and Community Events: These are like the singles cruises of dating—you can reach a whole group of potential customers at one time and in one swoop. Consider your clientele, and then choose trade shows and events that attract these people. These events can also help build your reputation and visibility.

PART 2: Attract Clients Like Honey to a Bee

5. Social Media: Can you think of anyone who doesn't have a smartphone these days? What about Facebook? Having an online presence is essential, and social media is an often free, easy way to reach large numbers of potential clients (online dating anyone)? This section will take you through the major social media platforms/channels and give you insider secrets on how to use them to get an edge on your competition.

6. Traditional Advertising: Sometimes, the old-fashioned ways work—reaching out to potential clients via advertising on the TV and radio, in newspapers and magazines, through the mail, etc. This section will highlight each of these media and help you determine whether traditional is the way to go.

7. Sweetening the Deal: Promotions and Special Events

> **Use Promotions and Special Events to:**
> - Attract potential clients
> - Keep current clients satisfied
> - Woo back absent clients
> - Win over unhappy customers

Oh, the power of gifts and dates. Or, in the case of business, of promotions and special events.

This section is full of ideas to bring in potential clients as well as keep your current clients. We'll even discuss ways to woo back clients you haven't seen in a while or who've had a bad experience at your salon (it happens).

Just as sales draw people to a store, promotions and events draw people to salons, spas, and barbershops. In today's world, everyone is looking to save money, so it's up to you as their service provider to make their visit a fun, exciting, new, and—ultimately—memorable experience.

PART 3: Get Ahead of Your Competition

8. Be Business Savvy: Lots of people can style hair, but not a lot of people can run a business. To be successful and stay in business, you must also put on your business hat. This applies to all, from the stylists to the owner. Stylists and barbers need to be thinking all the time of ways to increase their books of business—it's not good if everyone's coming in to get their hair did by Rachel or Ross but not you. Mama salon or Papa barbershop is not going to spoon-feed you clients.

"Talent is cheaper than table salt. What separates the talented individual from the successful one is a lot of hard work."
—Stephen King

9. Think Outside the Box: This section will highlight potential clients you may not have considered. Just as in dating you have a "type," sometimes dating outside your type can land you the love of your life. In this case, though, your target clients may be hiding in places you haven't considered. Read this section for some out-of-the-box ideas for clients and where to find them as well as fun ideas to draw people to your salon/spa/barbershop. Some examples are accountants (yes, accountants), construction sites, and fraternities and sororities. (This doesn't mean attending keg parties to find clients. But, really, colleges abound with client opportunities. Read this section to find out.)

PART 4: Giving Back

10. Give Back and Show Support: "Let us not become weary in doing good . . ." the Bible verse says. It's a mystery that giving back yields rewards to the giver. This section provides tons of ideas to get involved in causes and organizations near and dear to you and your community. Help others and also promote goodwill in your community. These relationships can reap dividends that go beyond clients, but you will see your business grow when you start giving back. It's a mystery, but it works. What goes around comes around; it makes for good karma.

Implementation Guide

In this section, you'll see how to put it all together to plan an amazing promotional event. Many of the ideas in this book don't require a lot of time or money, but some will involve more detailed planning. The step-by-step process featured in this section will give you a framework to use when you plan your next event or promotion.

Conclusion and Speed Dating with Celebrity Stylists

Here you'll get a final pep rally from the authors and some personal advice from celebrity stylists (think speed dating)—final words to get you out there in the game to winning and keeping clients. We know you're going to FILL THAT CHAIR!

Dating (Client-Winning) 101:
How Winning Clients Is a Lot Like the Dating Game

First Impressions Count: Looks and Personality

"Some of us light up a room when we enter, others when we leave. Which one are you?"
—Jeff Grissler

In dating, both image and personality are important. Looks are only going to get you so far if there's nothing behind the perfect white teeth and impeccable hair. On the other hand, if you have a winning personality but dirty hair and smelly breath, you're not going to get called back for a second date.

The same holds true for finding clients to fill your chair.

First impressions count. You're in the beauty industry; your job is to make people beautiful (or handsome if you're a barber).

But think about it, would you want someone with a horrible haircut or dye job touching your precious mane? Or someone whose makeup looks like a 5-year-old took her mother's lipstick and drew it all over her face? Would you blame someone for not choosing your services if this were true of you?

You also want to come across as someone who knows what you are talking about. If you don't know the basic terms of hair or makeup (or whatever your beauty focus), why would someone want you to have at it with a pair of scissors and her very precious hair? Too, people stick with a stylist who makes them feel valued, a part of the family so to speak—who not only does a good job on their hair/makeup/etc. but who makes the salon experience a comfortable and pleasant one. Remembering details about your clients' lives and asking about their little Suzie so and so or their new job is the type of practice that wins clients for life.

Here are some tips to help you make that great first impression.

While we all have days our hair won't do what we want it to, or days we just can't figure out what to wear (and the bed or floor looks like a clothing bomb exploded), we must still remember that we are representing a worker in the beauty industry. So we should do our best to be on our A game each day we step out the door. Represent!

Dress for Success: The Looks Part

"If you look good, you feel good; if you feel good, you do good; if you do good, you win! Win your way to new clients, and keep the ones you have!"
—Jeff Grissler

Before you leave the house, even when running errands, fix your hair and put on a little makeup (ladies), or shave or comb your beard (gents). Wear neat, stylish clothes (not clothes so wrinkled it looks like you pulled them from the bottom of the hamper), and shine your shoes. Look the part of a beauty professional. This doesn't mean you have to wear tux and tails every time you go to the grocery store or the coffee shop, but maybe a nice, pair of jeans and a classy sweater or button-down.

Because everyone knows if you throw on those sweats, you'll see your prize potential client. Feel confident in what you're presenting to the world, and you won't be behind the soup can display, hiding from said prize potential client.

Style versus Trends

(excerpted from "Are You Stylish or Trendy? Canadian Fashion Gurus Draw the Line," Faze Media)

"Someone once said that fashion is what you're offered. Style is what you choose. Stylish people know themselves and what's right for them," says Jeanne Beker, star of Fashion Television and editor-in-chief of *FQ Magazine*. "They choose to dress in what they feel good in and what they adore. A trendy person simply follows the crowd."

While stylish people do pay attention to trends, they don't just copy what they see in a fashion magazine. Stylish people are not afraid to mix designer labels with secondhand and discount clothing. The television show *Sex in the City* started a lot of trends because the Sarah Jessica Parker character had a lot of style. She mixed clothes that weren't necessarily in or out of fashion.

"Trendy people want to show off their designer labels and logos. It's very important for them to establish themselves in a certain social milieu," [Montreal designer Philippe] Dubuc says. In contrast, stylish people might wear designer clothes, but they will wear them casually.

To some extent, stylish people are born with their fashion sense. "It's like a radar," [Toronto-based designer Sunny] Choi says. Style icons like Audrey Hepburn and Jackie Kennedy are examples of people with an innate sense of style.

These days you can express your style in different ways according to your mood on a particular day. Seeking out secondhand clothes and combing the racks of discount shops make take some time, but it's a great way to create a personal look without spending a lot of money. [1]

Walking Billboard
If you're a basketball player, you wear good sneakers. If you're a stylist, you wear good hair. If you do nails, your nails should be filed and painted. Consider yourself a *walking billboard* for your craft.

When in Doubt, Wear Black
You can't go wrong with black clothes. Black is classic, it's chic, and, best of all, it makes us look skinny. When in doubt, wear black.

Have a Positive Attitude, and Know What You and Your Salon/Spa/Barbershop Has to Offer: The Personality Part

"Learn more about what you do,
and customers will start to listen to what you have to say."
—Jeff Grissler

Know what you have to offer. Know what you can do with hair or makeup or facial hair—whatever your beauty skill. You are good. You know your stuff. When you meet prize potential client and she asks what you do, you'll know what to say.

"I work for __ salon/spa/etc., and I specialize in __. If you need __, __, or __, I'm your gal."

Even better if you're keeping up with your business's specials and if you're carrying business cards and coupons. (You'll learn more about these tools later.)

Newbies and New Grads, this is for you. Learn these lines by heart.

You Have to Ask: Put Yourself Out There

"You've got to ask! Asking is, in my opinion, the world's most powerful—and neglected—secret to success and happiness."
—Percy Ross

How do you get business without asking for it? You don't.

Have you ever wondered what makes some people more successful at business than others? Are they really that much better than you if they are doing the same thing? Are they more creative or better at their job? Did they attend a better cosmetology school? Were they mentored by the best of the best? Are the products they use simply better than yours, enhancing their execution and their overall performance? My guess is, most likely, no.

The big difference is that they do one thing better:
THEY ASK FOR BUSINESS.
Yes, it's that simple.

If you don't ask for business, you may never get any business.

To go back to the dating metaphor, how many people would be single and alone if they didn't simply ask for the first date, nerves and all? Without asking for business, you may never get what you want. In the case of this book, you're looking for customers. (If you're looking for a mate, hey, some of these tips may translate. But we'd advise heading to the Relationships section of the bookstore for that kind of advice.)

Customers mean you're busy. Busy means you're making more money. More money doesn't always make you happier, but it sure helps. We can't solve making you happy. That may be in the next book. But the goal of this book is to get you customers, fill your chair or book of business, and hopefully change your life.

Why It Doesn't Hurt to Ask

Let's look at life in general. Most of the people we see, touch, drive by, walk by, chat with, or have daily communication with have one thing in common: they have HAIR.

They need you. It doesn't matter what they do for a living, how much money they make, the car they drive, or where they live. They have hair, nails, a face, a beard, sore muscles, eyelashes, and body hair, and they need you—

the cosmetologist, barber, makeup artist, massage therapist, and nail tech. Open your eyes to the world, get out of your little box, get rid of your security blanket, stop whining, and when you leave the house each day, realize that each person you come in contact with that day can be a potential customer. Wow, is that possible? Yes, but it all comes down to you.

Yes, this may sound like a bad commercial, but let's look at the facts. We all have hair, it grows, and when we get older, it turns gray. Are you getting the point? Hair grows and turns gray. People need to get it cut and colored. Like we said before, they need you. It doesn't hurt to ask for business. They're going to someone to cut and color their hair, so why not make that person *you*?

A Wise Man Once Told Me a Story . . . Jeff's Hammer-on-the-Head Moment
Early in my career, I didn't have the business smarts nor the confidence to understand that although people may know what you do, talk to you daily, and like you as a person, it doesn't necessarily mean they will do business with you. I assumed that because they talked to me and it seemed that they liked me, they would automatically use my services and business.

Just because.

Even if they pick up the phone when you call, text you back, or answer you on Facebook, it doesn't mean they will be your customers. Don't assume. Learn to ask.

Wrong. What does the word *assume* do? Make an ass out of you and me? That's just not how it works in the real world.

People know people who know someone who cuts hair. They most likely have a relationship built with someone. Maybe that person is their aunt, uncle, niece, neighbor, daughter, or son. You're not the only stylist or barber on the planet.

My mentor and boss at the time, the owner of a major beauty distributor still around today, holding its own against today's major corporations, asked to have a meeting with me to review my sales numbers at his place of business.

He had his agenda, and I had mine. He wanted to know why my numbers, or should I say my book of business, hadn't grown in two years. I sold hair-care products. My business was flat, and I was in the same place I was when he hired me. (I had gone in to ask for a raise.) He wanted to cut my draw and lower my salary. Not a good position to be in. My next stop: unemployment.

He said to me, "I don't have to give you a raise; you can give yourself a raise just by asking people for business."

He said I was talented, a great people person, always dressed for game-on situations, that everyone liked me, but—and here is the big *but*—HE NEVER ONCE HEARD ME ASK FOR A SALE. Never once heard me ask someone to recommend me to a friend or family member. He never even heard me ask for a date. (I was very much single at the time.) Then, it hit me.

Wow, he was right. I never had the nerve to simply ask for business of any kind. I would go into a salon, know everyone's names, have coffee, share stories, laugh—they all liked me—but I never focused on why I was there. It would bother me that other manufacturers' products were on their shelves. Here I was missing the most important parts of business: asking for more business, assisting with education on why my products were better, and helping the salon owner sell my retail. That's why I was there, right? Duh!!!

That was my day of awakening. The realization hit home.

From that point forward, I would ask everyone that I could for business and referrals. This conversation, this piece of golden advice, changed my entire life and the way I lived in less than a year.

I realized that if you don't ask, you just assume, ponder, and say tomorrow is going to be better. Without a reason to change, everything just stays the way it is. You may be the best stylist or barber in the world, and, sure, some people may find you. But to truly make the money you need to live—better yet, *to prosper*—you just can't do it without asking.

This book is about mentoring you. If I could teach you just one thing out of these 164 ways to get business, the most important one and the easiest I'd teach is *learning how to ask for it*. It's that simple, and it doesn't cost you a penny.

Ask for business is lesson one. Try it. It will change your life.

And while you're at it, if you're single and ready to mingle, ask him or her out already. Okay . . . we'll leave the dating advice to the experts.

Are You Afraid You'll Have TOO MANY Clients?

Sometimes, the fear of success can prevent us from sharing our business with others. Perhaps you're afraid you won't be able to handle an influx of new customers. Perhaps it fills you with a sense of pressure.

If this is you, step back a moment and take a breather. Really, you have nothing to fear. You're in the driver's seat. Remember that little thing called an appointment book? Those little slots in it that tell you whether you can take on another client on a particular day?

If you're booked, you're booked. Set another appointment. Remember, when you're booked, it shows the other person you're *in demand*. This equals "This stylist/barber/esthetician/what have you must be GREAT. And I can wait another day or two. It's worth it."

And if you're booked, you're making money. If you're not booked, you're not making money. Simple as that.

You have nothing to fear. It will all work out. If you're too busy, hire an assistant, you can afford one now.

PART 1
Where to Find Clients

NETWORKING

"The opposite of networking is notworking."
—Jeff Grissler

Networking is the most cost-effective way to expand your business. All it takes are good social skills, a little time and a little money. But, most often, it's the FREE and EASY methods of winning clients; and it can be the most effective. This is because networking is about focusing on the *other* person. It's about being in tune with the needs, wants, and desires of the people you meet and how your product and service can meet those needs, wants, and desires.

As a cosmetologist or salon owner, you know that your products are needed and desired. Everyone needs a haircut, and everyone needs pampered now and again. Looking good is a confidence booster.

While networking can take place anywhere, it's important to ask yourself, Who are my target clients? Who would *best* benefit from what I have to offer? How do my services and products benefit this client? Then, you'll be more able to spot these potential clients when you see them and even put yourself in places where they're going to be. And, because you're prepared—knowing how your service or product will help—you'll know how to communicate with this client when you *do* cross paths.

This sounds like dating, doesn't it? You know, hanging out at the places where your crush hangs out, knowing something about him or her so you're not left speechless; then finally talking to them.

Say Thank You
Remember to thank your referral sources for their support of your business. A handwritten note is great, a Starbucks gift card is even better.

The Power of a Name

How valued do you feel when you go to the bank or the coffee shop and the worker knows your name, knows your usual, and asks about your kids or your job? It makes you feel good, yes? You are more than a number. You are a person. And doesn't it make you want to return to this place of business? Keep this in mind. Get to know people. Remember names and a few details about their lives. Build relationships. This is the way to win *clients for life*.

Networking, Time and Money, Potential Investments

Time
- Time to create marketing materials
- Time to make a list of people to reach out to
- Time to reach out to them (in person, phone, letters, email)
- Time to attend events or join groups where these people gather

Money
- Travel expenses
- Stamps and postage
- Marketing materials
- Business cards
- Printing costs
- Service giveaways (they cost your time and money)
- Subscription to papers or magazines to keep up with local events
- Admission or donation for events
- Membership dues

Have a Stack of Business Cards on You at All Times

Yes, those old-fashioned paper thingies with your name and contact information on them.

> *"Rock stars get room keys, I get business cards."*
> —Thomas Friedman

So why should we use business cards when most of us have smartphones with fancy storage systems that can hold anything? Heck, we can even find the website of the salon and bookmark it right then and there.

Here are eight reasons business cards STILL RULE:

- It's easier and quicker to just whip out a business card rather than trying to plug all that information into your phone.
- Having a business card makes you look more professional.
- Business cards represent you and your salon and show off your personality and the image you want to project.
- Things get lost in phones. It's likely the person will forget where they put your salon information. In the Notes? What was her name again? Did I put her name under the name of the salon? What's the name of the salon?
- Business cards are still treated with respect and value. Most people keep them.
- Use your cards for more than just contact information. On the back, put a call to action, something that will prompt customers to come in. Offer $5 off your next service, a discount on retail, or something similar to get them in your chair.
- They're not expensive to make. Ask your salon/spa/barbershop if employees can have them made through the business. If not, there are tons of places offering business cards at cheap rates—Vistaprint, for example. You can also print them on your own printer or have them made at a printshop or an office supply store.

Ready for your first tip? Sorry it took so long, but get ready to book your chair solid.

TIP 1

Friends and Family: Aunt Sally and Uncle Hugh

In our quest to fill our chairs, we may forget the obvious people—those who love us and want to see us succeed: our friends and fam. Sure, Cousin Jo may have memories of you cutting her Barbie's hair into a mullet, but now, armed with your cosmetology degrees, and super scissor skills, you can prove her wrong.

Your friends and family may already have their own favorite stylists, but that doesn't mean they won't give you a try or recommend you to their friends. You are blood, after all. But in the midst of their busy schedules, they may need to be reminded that you're out there, standing in your sweet-smelling salon, scissors and comb in hand, ready to make people beautiful.

Make a list of all your friends and family who live within, say, a thirty-minute radius of your salon. Then, pick up that phone and call those friends and family. Let them know you'd love to give them a free consult and show them around. Ask if they have anyone you can invite in for a free consult. Take advantage of family parties to talk about your passions in hair, makeup, or whatever you do at said salon. And remind them, "Hey! You still get that free consult. Would really love if you came in, Cousin Jo."

For those of you who have been out in the field working in a salon, spa, or barbershop for a few years or if you own a salon, it doesn't hurt to remind your next of kin, friends you haven't seen in a while, or your long lost lover what you do and where you are in life. Remember, ask and you shall receive a former customer or a new one.

TIP 2

The People You See at Work: And There Are Many More Than You Think

---

New to the beauty game? Read this chapter immediately.

Think of people you come in contact with daily or even once or twice a year. They are all potential customers and referrals.

The Mailman
This person visits your business EVERY SINGLE DAY. If you're not cutting his or her hair, WHAT ARE YOU WAITING FOR? Heck, cut it for free; think of how many people the letter carrier touches every day. Through wind, hail, snow, and rain, this person could spread the word faster than you can! And talk about a walking billboard! *Oh, you like my hair? Thanks! Suzie at X, Y, Z Salon cut it for free!*

Here's a list of potential customers to get your wheels turning. Some of these may seem to apply only to business owners, but consider that your salon may get a remodel or need repairs so these people may come into play even if you're an employee.

- Lawyer
- Builder
- Architect
- Trade workers (like electricians)
- Product distributors/vendors
- Accountant/bookkeeper
- Banker
- Delivery people

- Interior designer
- Cleaning service
- Web designer
- Graphic designer
- Sign person
- Printshop
- Restaurant where everyone orders lunch
- Mailman
- FedEx and UPS drivers
- Event caterers
- Flower shop
- Baristas from favorite coffee shop
- Phone service provider
- Internet provider

Check out the list and come up with a list of your own.

You get the gist. So many potential clients. Why are they potential clients? Here are five good reasons:

- They have hair. Or beards. Or nails. EVERYONE could use your services.

- All of them could use some pampering.

- You are building a relationship with them, even if they're only seeing you once or twice a year, and they want to see you succeed (unless you are rude to them, which of course you aren't).

- Since you're paying them and they're working for you, they feel obligated to pay you back. It's an "I'll scratch your back if you scratch mine" situation.

- They have friends and family who could use your services. Personal referrals are the best ones.

Give these individuals some business cards and salon menus. Ask them to spread the word or give out coupons to give to their loved ones. (Get ideas on some great promos in the section ***Sweetening the Deal: Promotions and Special Events.***)

Don't Be Desperate!

This doesn't mean pushing and shoving your fellow stylists as you both try to win the affections of the electrician coming in to fix your lights, big red dollar signs of love in your eyes. No, this is simply about *utilizing every opportunity*. As you're getting to know these people just let them know, that you're always looking for clients and have some openings if they know of anyone looking for a stylist. Have business cards and coupons ready to give them.

The easiest potential customer to turn into a regular is someone you know. Everybody is a prospect, it's up to you to make them a regular.

TIP 3

Past Jobs: *As Long as You Didn't Say "Goodbye Suckas!" When You Left*

What about your old coworkers? Who cuts their hair, does their nails, provides their beauty treatments? It could be you.

Again, these are people who know you, and, just like your friends and family, they'll want to support you and help you in your new ventures. People change jobs all the time, and often, these coworkers were our friends, even if we've lost touch.

Reach out to individuals with a friendly greeting and a coupon, and if you do it through an email or text, call them to follow up. If you left a previous workplace on good terms, stop by for lunch or at coffee break with a stack of business cards, salon or spa menus, and coupons (this works even better if you come baring donuts).

Make a list of all your previous workplaces and volunteer organizations. Could you pay them a visit? Reach out to certain individuals? Make a list and then pound the pavement, phone, and email.

TIP 4

Former Teachers: Let Them See the Fruits of Their Labors

Yes, why not? These folks invested blood, sweat, and tears into getting you through high school and training you to be the amazing stylist you are today, so why not let them know you've started a new job at X, Y, Z Salon and you'd love for them to stop by and bring a friend.

This also applies to all types of teachers, mentors, coaches, or anyone with whom you had a good relationship.

Make a list of your favorite teachers and reach out. Pay them a visit or drop them a line. At the very least, send them a business card and a note, letting them know where you've landed in life.

TIP 5

Connect the Dots: Reaching the Winners

Is there a target client you're trying to reach? Perhaps a business full of people who would come to your salon? Connect the dots and get after the winners, your ideal clients. Take advantage of the connections you already have. If you have friends or family members who interact with these people, you have more of an "in" than if you did a cold call or walk-in. Being personally vouched for goes far. This is gold.

Target Client
Where do your target clients live? work? play? If you know someone connected to these places and people, reach out and get a recommendation.

TIP 6

Places You Go to All the Time—The *Cheers* Principle: Where Everybody Knows Your Name

Think about all the places you go to on a regular basis—coffee shops, the gym, restaurants, stores, banks, libraries, your kid's school, day care, sports events. You get the picture. Places where everybody knows your name and they're always glad you came.

The point is, these people KNOW you. And most will like you and want you to succeed unless you cussed them out for getting your order wrong or booed their kid on the soccer field. Remember, too, that you are helping businesses by frequenting theirs, so why shouldn't they give yours a try? It's a win.

If it's a business, ask for some of their business cards to share, and would they mind sharing yours? Or letting you put up a flyer or a stack of business cards? If it's an individual you see on a regular basis—a person you see at the gym each morning, a parent you sit next to at your kids' sporting events—ask if you can give them a few business cards. Say you'd love to give their friends a free consult (or discount) and a free service to them for helping you out.

Embrace the opportunity. Beyond friends and family, these are people you've built relationships with. You are familiar to them and you're helping their business, so why wouldn't they want to help yours?

TIP 7

Your Regular Coffee Shop

We felt this deserved its own category because COFFEE IS EVERYTHING. Pretty much everyone drinks coffee or those teas with the fancy Zen names.

I think all of us have stopped in a coffee shop. Starbucks has at least three to five people working at all times. Introduce yourself to your local baristas (the people who make the coffee), give them your cards, and offer a free service. Baristas, if you haven't noticed, are typically very creative people—in touch with style and trends—working this job so they can pursue their own creative careers. Ask if you can put up a flyer or keep a stack of business cards near the cream-and-sugar area (you can buy a little plastic cardholder at any local office-supplies store).

The more you go to a place, the more you become like family. Haven't you seen *Cheers* reruns? (Yes, that show again.) Or what about *Friends*? Every sitcom has its coffee shop (*Friends*) or bar (*Cheers*) or diner (*Seinfeld*). You'll start to know the regulars and feel more comfortable handing over your card, letting them know you'd love to give them a free consult. If you think someone would look great with bangs or a layered cut, offer a free service. If you're talking to a tired new mom, offer a mani or pedi. To the regulars and the baristas, you'll become Ms. Suzie Salon or Mr. Harry Haircut and the first person who pops in their minds when a coffee customer asks, "Hey, do you know of any good salons in town? I just moved here . . ."

TIP 8

The Bank: Don't Be Afraid of The Suits

The bank is another place we all visit regularly. We get to know the tellers, managers, and even the regular customers on a first-name basis so why not hand out some coupons and business cards? What about getting involved in their promotions for new account holders? Perhaps you could partner with the bank to offer a free salon service or freebie to new account holders in exchange for the publicity. Remember, just ask.

TIP 9

Schools and Day Care

Schools, day care, and after-care centers can be great avenues for new clients. You may already be there with your own kids, or you can pop in sometime after the morning rush. Of course there are parents to invite to your salon, but what about office staff and teachers?

While office staff will not be able to share contact information, they may be willing to give families your welcome kit, coupon, or salon menu at registration. Also ask about prom and how you can get in on that action (maybe don't phrase it exactly like that). Besides the dress, hair and makeup are super important for this most important night of high school (beyond graduation, of course). Talk to the drama and choir teachers about their school plays and whether they'd be interested in having you be their hairstylist and makeup artist.

Be sure to reward admin and staff for any referrals.

Dances
Schools have so many dances, and guys and gals want to look STYLIN'. Of course, there's prom, but what about homecoming, spring and winter formals, and themed dances? Be the "IT" salon for students.

STUDENTS
Students are an often-overlooked client. With their social media savvy, they'll spread the word for you.

TIP 10

The Kiddos: Being a Parent Can Actually Pay You for Once—with Clients

Let's think beyond school to all the ways your kids can bring you clients. What do we mean by this?

When you become a parent, you become part of a group consumed by your kids: feeding times and potty training, cartoons and books, naptimes and playdates become the topic of every conversation. When you're talking to other parents at day care, sports groups, the bouncy-house, take the time to connect, introduce your business and invite them in.

Parents are tired, so invite fellow parents into your salon for a cut and color, facial, mani/pedi—basically, some good old-fashioned pampering. They deserve it. Be the one to pamper them and earn their long-term business.

These are your people.

Brainstorm all the places you take your children, all the places you could connect with parents—then let them know you'd love them to come to your salon for an afternoon of pampering—"We're having specials all month in __." Or, "Here's a coupon. Stop by for a visit."

TIP 11

Church: Still the Best-Dressed Day of the Week

Church—or the services at whichever temple, mosque or meditation center you attend—is a social element, from the days when you come together to pray and worship to all the social events your spiritual family puts on, there are plenty of opportunities to nework and promote your business.

Get excited, talk about your passions in hair, makeup, makeup, and beauty with your spiritual family. Let your community know you're looking for clients. Have business cards on hand. Perhaps even hold a beauty event in the social hall, handing out coupons and cards at the end.

Think about it, most of us still put on our best outfits to attend worship services, so looking good is always on our minds. In many ways, it's an ideal place to find clients, but remember to always be respectful of your spiritual community's beliefs and practices when it comes to modesty and gender roles.

Jot down all the ways to connect with people in your place of worship, and bring business cards and coupons to all these events. These are people you've built relationships with, and you're all there to support each other. Show support for them and their endeavors, and let them show support for yours.

TIP 12

Rethink the After-Work Routine—Put Down the Remote and Ice Cream

It's so easy after a hard day behind the chair or managing a salon to arrive home in a bad mood—cranky, depressed, and frustrated that things are slow at work. Many of us will indulge in a martini (or three), a glass (or bottle) of wine, bowl of ice cream (or the container).

No matter what the routine of choice when you get home—booze, TV, radio, junk food, mindless book—we call this a *routine for disaster*. This dull, predictable habit in no way motivates you for a more productive, happier tomorrow, and it certainly won't help solve your problems. Yes, you may be relaxed, but sitting home drinking wine, eating bonbons while watching sitcoms, or playing on your mobile device is a dispirited way to show you want to advance your career and improve your customer base.

How do you change these habits? There's a lot of talk in the psychology world about creating routines that help us transition from the stresses of work to a happier evening. What about choosing better routines? Join a gym, yoga class, book club, singles group, political group, volunteer, take up bowling or volleyball, just GET OUT OF THE HOUSE. And carry your cards; tell people what you do, and ask for business.

TIP 13

Doctors' and Dentists' Offices

There is no way to avoid the doctor and the dentist. Since everyone has to go, why not kill two birds with one stone? While there, you probably talk with at least five people if not more. Start with the receptionist. She is asking for your information, right? Everything about you including your profession, right? You have to write it, and you also have to give your insurance card, right? So why not give her your business card? Speak to each of the people working there, including your doctor and the assistants (the people who weigh you and take your X-rays and blood pressure), and tell them about what you do and how great you are as a stylist. If you see any bored-looking folks in the waiting room (um, EVERYONE), engage them in a conversation as well. If you own the salon, offer a discount for a first visit; if you rent a chair, offer up a free styling with a cut. Hand out some coupons.

TIP 14

Accept All Social Invites: Go to Things

By just attending events and being social, you are helping your business. Attending business networking and charity events, parties of friends and family, and galas are all excellent ways of creating a bigger client base. Most local papers have a "What's Happening This Week" section that lists upcoming events, if it doesn't, check your local Craigslist for community events or browse Meetup.com's activities for your area. Get in the habit of checking it regularly and attending events that have your target clients. And accept any invitations to social events. Unless you're fried with commitments or down with a raging stomach flu, social events are a prime way to meet new people—all potential customers.

Remember, at these events you are representing your work and the salon, so take some time to style your hair and look the part. Game on!

Top Ten Tips for Rocking an Event

1. **RSVP.** If the event requires an RSVP, make sure you do so.

2. **Dress appropriately.** If the event says "formal," "white tie," or "cocktail attire," make sure you dress appropriately. If you're not sure what the dress code is, just ask. Better to overdress than to look like you don't belong. You can always take off a layer.

3. **Highlight your top skills.** If you're a top-notch hairstylist, style your hair to the nines. If you're a makeup artist, do your makeup impeccably. If you're a barber and sport a beard, make sure it's trimmed nice, tight, and looking right. Be creative and stand out—but in a good way. Have some pics on your phone should a guest want to see more of your work. At the very least, give your business card so he or she can come in the salon for a free consult or a discounted or free service. y

4. **Bring something.** You will win the first-impression rose if you bring

a good bottle of wine or delicious food to a party. Bring the hostess a small gift. If it's a charity event, make a donation.

5. Bring lots of business cards. Share with people you're talking with; ask if you can have theirs as well.

6. Be genuinely interested in people. Just talk to them. Don't be the girl or guy going from person to person trying to "sell something." Now, if the event is a clear networking event, this is fine. Still, show some interest and be a good listener before busting in with, "Can I tell you about my salon?"

7. Don't drink too much. 'Nuff said.

8. If you're there until the end, offer to help clean up. Always clean up your own mess and any cups or plates around you, taking cups back to the kitchen and throwing your trash away. And always say goodbye to the host with a warm thank you.

9. Send a thank you card to the event host within a week of the event. This should be an actual card made of paper. An email or text is nice, but an thank you card stands out. Plus you can slip another business card or coupon inside.

10. Follow-up with the people you met. Email, text, or Facebook message the people you met and tell them how wonderful it was to meet them, let them know where you work, and offer a discount on a service at your salon.

For Those on a Budget
Don't bring out the charge card for new duds, no need. There are plenty of rent-a-dress or rent-a-tux companies—whether bridal shops in town or online businesses, such as Rent the Runway—that allow you to rent fancy duds at a much lower cost than buying.

TIP 15

Join the Chamber of Commerce . . . Don't Be Afraid to Admit You Don't Know What It Is; Just Read on!

This is a huge resource that many businesspeople don't take advantage of. Heck, many of us don't even know what it is, but it's simple: the Chamber of Commerce is just a collection of local businesses.

Sign up to become a member of your local chamber, and attend its networking events. The chamber will enable you to introduce yourself to local businesspeople and new people in the community.

People who are new to town often contact the chamber for recommendations for housing, doctors, restaurants, and attractions—even hair salons. Ask the chamber if you can put a salon menu and coupon in their new-resident packets. Most people think highly of Chamber of Commerce members. Since the Chamber is a trusted network, they trust you.

There will likely be dues for membership and sometimes for sponsored networking events. Dues for chamber membership vary depending on the size of your business and where you live. At times, dues can be costly, but save up and join for a year; during that year, track your Chamber business and if it doesn't make you money, chalk it up as an experiment that was less-than-successful.

Remember, with any business investment, you must track your success to see if it is worth the cost.

TIP 16

Join and Attend Business Networking Groups and Events

Tons of business networking organizations exist beyond the chamber of commerce. To find these, check out local papers and magazines, do some Internet searching, and visit sites like meetup.com.

There are all types of business networking organizations:

- **Casual Contact Networks**—Like the chamber, these are collections of different types of business owners who meet monthly.
- **Strong Contact Networks**—These groups are focused on referrals, so usually only one member from each profession or specialty is allowed per group; in these groups, networking is welcomed and expected.
- **Community Service Organizations**—These are groups like Kiwanis, The Elks, Rotary and similar groups. These organizations are often full of local businesspeople.
- **Professional Associations**—Ask your target/best clients if they belong to any professional organizations, and look into how you can make connections through this group.
- **Social/Business Organizations**—There are lots of meet-up groups for business professionals that combine social activities with networking; check out www.meetup.com.
- **Women's Business Organizations**—These are often focused on networking and professional development; some also try to keep membership focused to one person per profession or specialty. [1]

TIP 17

Join Anything! (Book Club, Shuffleboard, Skee-Ball Group, Knitting Group, Monday Night Poker Club—Whatever Floats Your Boat)

Join something that interests you, it doesn't necessarily have to be a business group: think social groups, charities, fitness clubs, book clubs, fundraising organizations, poker nights with the guys—whatever floats your boat.

Getting involved allows you to build relationships with a group of people around shared interests. Naturally, you will want to support people you know and care about; you'll want to support their ventures, and they'll want to support yours. And when people ask your groupmates if they know a good salon or hairstylist, you'll be the first name they think of. Clients can follow naturally just from getting involved with organizations and building relationships.

Check out www.meetup.com, www.charitychoices.com, www.craigslist.org, www.lic.org (Local Independent Charities of America), www.volunteermatch.org, and www.unitedway.org for ideas.

Many groups are free to join while others may have membership dues. Some may ask you to bring drinks or desserts to meetings or require you to buy a book. Still, the relationships you build are worth it, and word-of-mouth sales are still the best ones.

TIP 18

Your Day Is Full of Opportunities—or Are You Missing Them?

Think of all those places you go in a typical day, from morning until evening. And think about all the potential clients you are walking by, driving by, and having contact with each day.

Are they opportunities or missed opportunities?

Let's take a look at a typical day for me. Call it Jeff's Friday.

I drove my daughter to *school*. While there, I had to drop off something in the office, which meant I was greeted by the secretary, other office workers, and the principal. I also bumped into a few parents of my daughter's friends.

Opportunity or Missed Opportunity?

I drove to *Starbucks* where I saw my favorite barista, Julia, who fixed me up my favorite coffee. I told her I liked her necklace, that it was very creative. She told me she makes jewelry.

Opportunity or Missed Opportunity?

After my caffeine fix, I headed to the *gym*. The gym was full of people who take pride in their appearance, enough to squeeze in time in their busy workday. I know the trainers, and the same people are there every day working out (I know most by their first names).

Opportunity or Missed Opportunity?

Postworkout, I headed to the *bank* to deposit a few checks. While there, I was waited on by Kathy, who's waited on me before. I asked about her day, whether she had any fun plans for the weekend. There were a few other tellers milling about as well.

Kathy knows I grew up in New York City, and she asked me if I knew

any good restaurants there because she was going there with her family. I recommended a few.
Opportunity or Missed Opportunity?

Next was the *post office* where I had to mail a package to a client. I stood in a line of maybe five or six people just twiddling their thumbs or mindlessly scrolling through their Facebook feeds.
Opportunity or Missed Opportunity?

After the post office, I drove to work. Can you count up the potential customers I had already come across that morning—even before I made it to work?

Everyone gets a haircut. Everyone wants to look good. Everyone is looking for a good deal.

Was the morning full or opportunities or missed opportunities?

Okay, so if you didn't take advantage of the morning, what about the afternoon? The evening?

Lunchtime rolled around, so I headed out to the local *sandwich shop*. Once again, I stood in a line of maybe five or six people before reaching the cashier and sandwich maker—two young people, maybe early twenties—one with spiky black hair poking out under his hat, the other with multiple rings. Clearly, they were trying to show their individuality despite the fact they have to wear corporate aprons and hats.
Opportunity or Missed Opportunity?

After lunch, stomach full and happy, I finished out my workday and picked up my daughter at *school*, again seeing a few parents I recognized as well as some teachers directing students to buses.

We then stopped by the *library* so she could pick up a book for a project, and then I drove her to a *piano lesson*, waiting in the lobby with a couple of other parents.
Opportunity or Missed Opportunity?

After that, we went to the *grocery store* to pick up food for dinner; while there, we went to the deli, the bakery, said hello to some neighbors, and stood in a line again.

Later on, after dinner, my kids out with friends, my wife and I decided to go to a local ***restaurant*** for a glass of wine and adult conversation. It was Friday night. We deserved it. We had freshened up and put on some nice duds. We looked classy, like we knew style. Even the waitress commented on how nice we looked. Other Friday nights we'd be at our son's ***football games***, cheering him on with hundreds of other parents, family members, and friends—many whom we'd gotten to know just by sitting with them many Fridays.

Opportunity or Missed Opportunity?

I could keep going, but you get the drift.

Action Step
Take five minutes and jot down a list of all the potential places you go during the week and all the people you see. Think about all the potential customers you come across, all wanting to look and feel their best, all needing beauty services. Are these people your customers? They should be.

Consider, too, that you've built relationships with many of these people already. You are a familiar face. There's no awkwardness. No sleaziness to telling them (or even people you're meeting for the first time) about services you believe will make them look and feel their best. You're spending money on *their* services, so why wouldn't they try *yours*?

"Those who are blessed with the most talent don't necessarily outperform everyone else. It's the people with follow-through who excel."
—Mary Kay Ash

The best thing about networking is that it often takes zero time and zero money. You're there already. You're just embracing the opportunity.

So don't miss it. These people know you, like you, and trust you, but they may have no idea what you do for a living. Tell them next time you see them, and don't forget to do one thing: ASK! Yes. Ask them to come by and give you and your salon a try. Remember the old expression. Well, if you never heard it, here it goes: IT NEVER HURTS TO ASK! Visualize yourself telling Bridget the Barista about your business and handing her your card and a coupon. Now put on that game face and get out there, tiger.

Five Essentials for Networking Success

1. **Always have business cards** on you. Keep them in your purse, briefcase, or pocket. Be prepared.

2. **Play connect the dots.** Even if you're not the right guy or girl for the job, connect people to the person who is. You'll be known as trustworthy and helpful, and it will come back to you.

3. **Be genuinely interested** in the other person. Don't be a robot; get to know people. Have genuine conversations. Listen to them. Ask friendly questions. People love to talk about their kids, sports, favorite restaurants, etc. Remember, too, that the more you know about a person, the more you know how you can help him or her.

4. **Give more than you expect to receive.** If you want to build trust with your network, give more. Don't be needy, desperate, or stingy. When people see you as a person going above and beyond to help, they'll want to reciprocate and connect with you.

5. **Always follow up.** A quick email, text, or phone call within 24 hours of meeting someone can make a world of difference. Tell the person how nice it was to meet and how you'd love to give a free consult or discount on his or her next haircut or mani/pedi. The same goes for people in your network whom you haven't heard from in a while; reach out and ask them how they're doing, and offer a freebie or discount.

FORM PARTNERSHIPS

"The quality of your life is determined by the quality of your relationships. The quality of your business is no different."
—Harvey Mackay

You need clients to make money. The more you have, the more money you make. This applies to everyone, from the stylist to the salon owner. And not only do *you* need clients but the businesses next door to you, around the corner, and down the street do as well.

Have you ever thought that maybe your neighbor is going through the same thing as you? My guess is he or she is *absolutely* going through the "need-more-business-today" mode. No business owner ever stops thinking about what business will walk through the door today, tomorrow, next week, next month, or next year.

So why don't you consider partnering with your neighbors? There are lots of ways you can help each other win more clients and more business.

Three Types of Partnerships

Host-Beneficiary Arrangement (or, in English, Get a Sugar Daddy!)

In this arrangement, the sugar-daddy arrangement—also called piggybacking (we're not making this up), you're loosely partnering with an established, successful business that has a solid reputation in the community—this is a business that could take you places. This business should also cater to your target customers (or a new demographic you are trying to reach). The host business might include an ad with a coupon for your salon/spa/barbershop in one of its newsletters or emails, or it might promote you via social media or in other ways.

With this type of arrangement, you'll need to show the host business the value of this partnership. Stress that it's a way for the host company to reward its clients in a unique way, promoting loyalty and goodwill. It also allows the host company to reach out to its clients in a helpful, non-sales-pitchy way.

You might offer to pay for mailing expenses, offer a commission on sales leads, or even barter for services.

Strategic Alliances (Long-Term Partners)

In this type of partnership arrangement, both parties benefit equally, and oftentimes, these partnerships are long-term. In these arrangements, partners might refer business to one another, share each other's promotions and plan events together.

This trust and mutual goodwill can also stir creativity and growth in business, as each is more willing to try new, innovative ideas.

A strategic alliance can take some time to develop as, over time, each of the two businesses sees how the partnership is beneficial. Sometimes, a host-beneficiary arrangement can blossom into a long-term, mutually beneficial strategic alliance.

With strategic alliances—two businesses mutually helping each other—costs are often shared.

Odd-Couple Partnerships (Opposites Attract)

These are unlikely partnerships that can yield big dividends—in part because no one else has thought of them before. Once they're formed, others will think, "Why didn't I think of that?" Benefits to unlikely partnerships are the absence of competition and the media attention that can occur with these unique, fresh ideas.

Brainstorm with your staff a couple of unique partnership ideas, and try out one or two of them. What about partnering with a prominent tax accountant in the area, offering him or her a free service and covering the marketing costs to include a coupon for tax-time sanity services to its clients? What about partnering with a shoe store, offering discounts on foot massages and pedicures? The possibilities are endless, and these partnerships may not only yield clients but also be a lot of fun.

In some cases, the value of mutually promoting each other's businesses is clear, an arrangement that could lead to a steady stream of referral business.

While some partnerships are short-term or one-off arrangements, others have long-term potential. Think about dating; some are just a summer thing while others have long-term relationship (LTR) potential. And some partnerships can be so good that they lead to a "marriage" of sorts.

Whatever the level of partnership, working with other businesses really helps. We're not meant to do it alone.

In the case of business, it's okay to have multiple partners and shared clients.

Four Things to Ponder Before Forming a Partnership

When considering partnerships, don't leap blindly, running from business to business shouting, "Will you be my friend?" Just as in friendship and dating, consider whether the relationship will be beneficial to you both. Here are four things to ponder when choosing businesses to partner with:

1. Who are my target clients? Where do these clients shop or eat? What do they do for fun? Are they close to your place of business? Try to keep it close to home.

2. Consider your current clients. Would they benefit from this partnership? If you're a boutique salon, don't think you want to start doing guy's fades and trendy beards.

3. Find partners that make sense. If you're a Men's salon, partner with a men's boutique or trendy bar or restaurant; if you cater to little old ladies, partner with businesses they frequent.

4. What are your goals for the partnership? Do the potential benefits outweigh the investment of time and money?

First Things First
First things first, see if you have any personal connections to the potential partner. Blind dates usually suck, so it's better to go in being introduced.

Partnerships
Time and Money
Potential Investments

Time

- Time to make a list of potential partners
- Time to reach out to these businesses (frequent their place of business)
- Time to plan events and promotions with your partners
- Time to put together a digital portfolio to show potential partners
- Time to put together marketing materials to leave with partners
- Time to follow up with potential customers

Money

- Subscription to papers that keep you in touch with local events
- Money for treating them to coffee or a meal
- Hostess gift
- Donation if it's a charity event
- Donation of products for a partner event
- Marketing materials to leave at partner businesses
- Cost of discounted or free services
- Any referral fees/cut of the proceeds you give to your partner
- Related costs for planning an event or promotion with your partners

---

Bring a Picture Portfolio
Choose your partners wisely. You have to be a match. It's like dating: if you're a 10, you don't want to partner with a 6.

POTENTIAL PARTNERS

TIP 19

Big Names in the Community— Hook Up with These People!

Who are the big names in the community? Try to connect with a person who has clout in the community. They can give you pointers for finding business and can connect you to the right people. Reach out via phone or email, introducing yourself in a professional manner, and ask if you could meet for coffee or lunch. Your treat.

Have a few things in mind to talk about when you meet, but make sure to listen. And remember to send a thank you note after the meeting.

If this person invites you to another event, GO.

Pay for the "Date"!
Treat the person you are inviting to coffee or lunch. This is an **investment**. If you are invited to an event, remember to bring a hostess gift, food item or bottle of wine if asked, and/or charity donation if it's a charity function. Even big shots like free stuff.

TIP 20

Local Hotels That Don't Have a Salon or Spa

Visit the local hotels that do not have in-house salons, and offer discounts to their guests if they have services done in your salon. Offer quick fixes, blowouts, makeup, color touch-ups, and nail repairs in addition to full services/packages for hotel visitors. Hotel guests are often looking for salon services, and when guests ask, the concierge would much rather provide a solution by sending them to your salon versus telling them, "Sorry, we don't have one." You may also want to offer the hotel staff or management a free service or a referral fee as a thank you. Make sure you bring any salon brochures/menus you have as well as some business cards.

You could gain tons of new clients with hotel partnerships—people on vacation are in the mood to spend a little money to be pampered.

Rainy Days Are a Good Thing!
Rainy days are a perfect day to hit the salon. Hotel management could have something written in their hotel materials about your salon and can suggest on such rainy days, "How about trying out 'Sunshine Salon'? It's a good day to have your hair or nails done, yes? A good day for some TLC."

You'll need to make a list of all the hotels in the area and then take some time visiting to each. You'll want to speak in person with the hotel owner or manager or arrange a time to meet at his or her earliest convenience to discuss a potential partnership. Put aside an afternoon each week to drive around and meet with hotel owners/managers.

TIP 21

Tanning and Nail Salons
(Partner with Them, or Start Offering These Services)

Most tanning or nail salons don't offer services for hair, skin, or makeup. What a great way to share their clients and yours. Recommend these partner beauty businesses, and start sharing clients today. Speak to the owner and coordinate a shared email campaign with both their customer list and yours. It's a great way to cross-pollinate your customer bases. Tweet your customers and let them know about your business partnership. Make sure the tanning or nail salon has your salon's menu and business cards.

> If you don't have tanning or nail services in your salon, add them. These can be real money-makers—think spray tans.

You'll need to make a list of the tanning and/or nail salons in the area and then pay a visit to each. Talk to the salon's manager or owner and arrange a time to meet to discuss a potential partnership. Put aside an afternoon each week to drive around to these businesses, before long, you'll have visited every one.

> **Spray Tanning!**
> Spray tanning is a cost-effective way to gain new clients. If you have a spare room turn it into a handheld spray-tan room. It costs anywhere from $1,000 to $1,500 to buy the spray gun and solution to get started. You can charge up to $45 for each spray tan you do on a customer; this will add up quickly. Cha-ching! Cha-ching!

TIP 22

 ## Gyms, Yoga, and Pilates Studios Attract Attractive People

The local gyms and fitness studios are more potential businesses to collaborate with. The people who go to these places care about their appearance and looking their best, they're ideal clients. Talk to them about a business card exchange: you keep a stack of their cards at your front desk and they do the same for you. You can also engage in an email campaign or announce via social media your partnership, offering discounts for first-time clients, a freebie if the individual mentions the promotion, or a 5 to 10 percent discount on each visit for members of the gym or studio.

You could even have an instructor from the gym or studio come in to teach your clients some exercises for stress relief. Maybe you could spend a few hours at the gym offering some easy services—how about mini facials, bang trims, or shaves? Have lots of cards and salon/barbershop menus on hand as well as promotional freebies with your business's name on them.

Make a list of all the fitness centers in the area, and then take some time driving to each. You'll want to speak face to face with the manager or arrange a time to meet at his or her earliest convenience to discuss a potential partnership.

Business cards work, but a small sign is even better. You can one made wherever your got your business cards.

TIP 23

Dance Studios and Dance Moms

Visit local dance studios and meet the owners. Dancing has always been popular, but with shows like *Dance Moms*, the studios are swarming with moms and their daughters all looking to be the next superstars. Offer to assist during dance competitions with getting the girls ready to compete.

Many of these studios have six competitions in one season. Offer to do the hair for the girls when competition season starts. This is a great way to get many of the moms and daughters into your salon. Ask, too, if you could have your name and the salon's name listed in the competition program.

Before you head out to visit each of the studios, check their schedules and the competition dates to see that your schedule is clear. When you visit, do so at a time when you can speak to the owner or head instructor about your partnership idea.

Bring a Picture Portfolio
Makeup and hair are a big part of dance competitions. Having a portfolio of pics to show off your work will greatly increase your chances of winning their trust and business.

Creative events like dance recitals may require some hairstyles or makeup looks that are outside of your comfort zone, so be sure you give yourself plenty of time to practice before the big day and to special order any tools or makeup (color extensions, color sprays, etc.).

This is why it's important to consult with the instructors to make sure you know what is expected. You're helping to bring their creative vision to life.

TIP 24

Theaters and School Productions: Hair and Makeup Make the Show

Similar to dance studios, local theaters and schools (from elementary school to college) need someone to do the actors' and actresses' hair. This is a chance for your talents to really shine. You could end up styling 1920s flapper hair or spinning beehives like cotton candy. If you've worked on a show before or have pics of unique hairstyles (or, better yet, ones that fit the production's time period), bring them along to the visit.

Digital Portfolios and Lookbooks
It's always good to have pictures of your work to show clients, so put together a digital gallery of your best looks. This is a great tool to win clients, especially when they have nothing to go on but your word. Look at other salon and fashion websites to get some examples of how to put together a gallery. Consider a site like **Bloom.com**, which allows you to have your own personal stylist profile and lookbooks that you can share via social media.

You may be told that the theater's budget is small or the school only accepts volunteers, so you'll need to think about whether taking a pay cut or volunteering is something you will do. Will the time you're investing be worth the promotions in the playbill and other materials put up around town? Will you win the loyalty of parents and school staff, who will start coming to you after the show?

> **Hey guys, don't forget about the playbill**—the little book that tells you all the actors in the play—it's a great place to get your name out there. If you're doing the hair or makeup for the show, see if they'll run an ad in it in exchange for your services; if not, a small ad will most likely be inexpensive.

Make a list of the theaters and schools in town. Finding the people in charge of productions may take a little digging. For schools, start with the drama and choir teachers (or, in doubt, ask the secretary). You can usually find their numbers on the school's website. They'll have all the info you need—production and dress rehearsal dates, show times, and, of course, their creative vision.

TIP 25

Restaurants and Health Stores

Here's a unique idea: partner with a local restaurant or health store. At farm-to-table restaurants, sushi and vegetarian eateries, co-ops, smoothie places, upscale bars and wineries—places that cater to fresh, healthy, and quality food—the customers take care of themselves. People love food; you could even host an event, a monthly happy hour perhaps, in which the partner business brings in samplers from its menu. Health stores might include samples along with a coupon. In turn, the business promotes your salon to its customers.

Do some research into the restaurants and health stores in town; it shouldn't be hard, you know all the hip spots to hang out, grab a drink, and get dinner. Sites such as yelp.com, tripadvisor.com, and restaurants.com, can help; your chamber of commerce should also have a directory. Make a list of ones you'd like to target. Discuss a potential partnership with the business manager of each.

TIP 26

Clothing Stores (Women's and Men's)

Consider a partnership with a clothing store, especially boutiques. You all want to make people look fabulous, so why not partner together and promote each other's businesses? Put on some fun events. With the whole beard trend, if you're a barber, you could do a demonstration in the clothing store showing guys how to style their beards for more upscale events. A salon and a boutique might plan a fashion show that showcases both the store's clothes and the salon's hair and makeup talents. There are tons of ideas here.

Make a list of clothing stores you love, or start driving around and browsing. Do any seem a good fit for a partnership? Would their clients feel at home in your salon? Do you have a similar vibe? Then, talk to the manager about a potential partnership. Ask if you could have coffee to discuss ideas.

Thank You Cards
Remember to send a thank you card to all the potential partners you've spoken with. **Even if one or the both of you decided a partnership is not in the stars, still send a thank you.** Who knows what the future holds, they'll remember you as a kind, polite individual and may end up referring you to others. Kindness is always a good thing, and classy manners are a rarity these days.

TIP 27

Realtors, Home Builders, Homeowner Associations, and Apartment Complexes: Reach the New People Before Anyone Else Does

Real Estate Agents and Home Builders

Partnering with real estate agents and home builders is a great way to get in the forefront of new residents. Provide "welcome-to-the-neighborhood" packages and coupons.

Homeowner Associations

Connecting with homeowner associations can be golden. Think of all the community center events, card games, and parties these groups host throughout the year. The communities with these types of organizations are the nice ones, ones in which the residents likely have some extra moolah. These could be good candidates for higher-end products, medical spas, blowouts, and frequent visits. Maybe you could do demonstrations for a community event, put gift cards in raffles, or hand out new-resident discount coupons for new-resident packages.

Apartment Complexes

If you live in a college town, you likely have lots of apartment complexes. Pick up an *Apartment Finder* or other local apartment guide (you can usually find these in coffee shops, grocery stores, and kiosks around town.)

New Developments

Pay attention to the new developments going up around town, and be the first salon to reach out to these new residents through a coupon mailing or new-resident package. You could even be part of the opening-day festivities. Often, radio stations broadcast the opening days of these larger developments, which means an even wider audience.

You can ask apartment managers and homeowner associations if they wouldn't mind including a salon postcard/coupon in their new-residents' packages, including you in their newsletter, or even putting something in resident mailboxes. You can ask if you could put a flyer up on the community bulletin boards and leave some business cards in the office (lots of places have a table full of local promotional items like coupons and cards). You could even leave some promotional materials for their community events and raffles.

Ask around if there are newcomers' groups sponsored by a civic group (like the Chamber of Commerce or local Visitors/Tourism Bureau or a religious group). Often these newcomers groups have speakers, mixers, and get-togethers where you may be welcome to come, introduce yourself, and plug your business. Even if they don't, the host or sponsor will typically provide newcomers with a welcome packet, so see how your salon, spa, or barbershop can be listed in there.

TIP 28

Small Business Development Centers

Small business development centers are excellent places to partner with. Professional appearance is essential to finding a job and landing clients. These organizations often sponsor professional etiquette and job-finding seminars, workshops, dinners, etc. See if you can provide tutorials on professional hair, grooming, and makeup. Sponsor an event, and have your salon listed in the marketing materials. Provide participants with coupons for a discount off their first visit.

TIP 29

Life and Business Coaches

Reach out to life and business coaches in your community. These individuals are helping people build their confidence and professional image, often to obtain a job. Be their referral salon! Provide some coupons, and maybe even plan and promote a professional-image event together.

 Not many people understand what these people do, hell, I don't even know. I think they're like your dad, they tell you what you're doing wrong and how to fix it. But, in this case, they may be a good lead source.

TIP 30

Dermatologists (The Money-Makers)

"To me, beauty and makeup and color is like the finishing touch on everything."
—Marc Jacobs

Ok, so you're an aesthetician. You love what you do, but the spa you work in just isn't busy enough. Remember, your destiny is in your own hands. Staying in a place just because it's convenient and/or because it's comfortable isn't the answer. Where you hang your hat is up to you. Make an appointment with a successful local dermatologist to see if you could work there or work with some of their clients. Not only could you be an aesthetician there and find extra work but you could also up your game with clients who are capable of having facials and skin-care work on a more frequent basis. Dermatology is often considered a luxury medical service, and clients coming there often have some extra spending money—they're not afraid to get facials and other treatments such as chemical peels. Most likely, they've had these types of services before, just not by you.

Interview with dermatologists who offer injectable and laser treatments for hair removal and/or collagen rejuvenation. These cater to people who are not having these services paid for by insurance. These clients will easily fork over $150 for a facial or skin treatment.

TIP 31

Home Parties: Partner with Friends Who Sell Things

If you have friends who do home parties (selling jewelry, nail polish, makeup, "intimate" items, Tupperware, etc.), why not partner with them and attend some of their events to meet a whole group of potential new clients? Give some facials and makeovers. Share insider tips. Hand out coupons, business cards, and salon menus. Have a rack of your friend's jewelry in your salon. Help each other out and both of you could have an instant group of potential new clients.

FUN PARTNERSHIP IDEAS

TIP 32

Collaborative Deals

Once you've tapped into partner relationships, collaborate with them for special deals. You could have a punch card good for a discount at each business one time—pick it up at any business, and use it at all the others.

Another way to collaborate is *with* your competitors. One example is $5 burger week in Toronto, when a group of restaurants collaborate to each offer fancy burgers for $5, advertising the event in local papers. How about a bunch of salons offering $10 haircuts and manicures for teachers the week before school starts?

You'll need to brainstorm some collaborative ideas and then meet with other businesses to get them on board. There's also the time involved in promoting the event and preparing any necessary materials (printing the punch cards, distributing them to the businesses, etc.). While there are a number of costs involved in planning a partnership event, these costs can be split. Consider, too, the many new customers you'll get in your chairs and how once they experience your mad styling skills, they'll be back and bring their friends—especially if you follow up with them.

TIP 33

Cross-Business Raffle

Fill a giant suitcase with fragrances, shampoos, free services, and as many contributions from your local business partners as you can. Have raffle tickets made, and get other businesses involved with the raffle. This will get other businesses and their customers familiar with your salon. You can call this cross-pollinating. The more people involved, the more people get stung. It's a win-win for your salon and staff and also for the other businesses in town. Don't forget to get your retail sales rep involved. He or she may offer up some free samples or discounted products for the raffle grand prize.

TIP 34

Co-sponsored Events and Seminars

If you share the same target audience with your partners, plan and promote a joint event. You'll be introduced in a more personal way to your partner's clients and we know that's always best. You'll save time and money by splitting the event work and marketing costs, plus joint events tend to garner more attention from the public and media.

You may decide to hold the event in one of your business locations or in a well-trafficked public place, such as a mall. Maybe you'll plan a wellness event with your fitness partners or a back-to-school event with your health food partner, having said partner give some easy, healthy brown-bag lunch ideas in your salon lobby while you cut the kid's hair for that very-important first day.

Gather Information!
Find some way to get the contact information of event attendees; perhaps have a raffle with space for names and emails on the back of the entry tickets.

Don't Be Afraid to Think Outside the Box
Who is your target audience? If you're a sports-themed barbershop, your partner may be the local sports bar down the street. Think about your target clients and where they spend their time. Then, see if you could build a partnership with their hangout's management.

TIP 35

Partner with a Wedding Planner

Who better to recommend a salon for the big day than a wedding planner? This is a terrific way to do a whole bridal party either in-house or at the wedding venue. Work out a barter system with the wedding planner or provide a referral fee. Offer discounts to the entire wedding party and their family. This is a wonderful way to attract new clients to the salon and your staff. Make sure you post the bride and her bridesmaids or groom and groomsmen on your social media sites. If it's okay with the bride and groom, tweet the world about the new couple getting married and you and your team doing their hair, makeup, etc.

Out Of Town Guests
Wedding Planners have the bride's ear, and can refer your services to the bridal party and any out of town guests. After all, Aunt Mary from Akron needs to have her hair done for the wedding.

TIP 36

Partner with a Photographer

Photographers who specialize in engagement and wedding photos are a great way to meet new clients. Let them recommend your salon to look gorgeous for the photos. You could even suggest the photographer use your salon for the shoot. Barter with the photographer for referral business. Post the pictures on social media and in your salon or salon's windows, making sure the photographer's name is prominent. Ask the photographer to give credit for hair and makeup in the photos they post. Make sure the photographer has your salon's menu and your business cards, and ask for theirs as well.

TIP 37

Partner with a Bridal Shop and Tux Rental

Bridal shops are a wonderful way to meet new clients. Work out a barter system or a referral program with the bridal shop's owner or salespeople. Have business cards and your salon's menu on hand at the bridal shop. Ask if you can leave a small photo book of bridal hair and makeup done by your salon; when brides find their perfect dress, they'll be able to envision the whole package—dress and hair and makeup. And they'll know whom to call!

Grooms want to look their best on their big day, too. Stop into some of the local tux places and ask if you can leave behind some materials—business cards and barbershop or salon menus. Include some pictures of sharply dressed and groomed guys in your menus/brochures—and hey, work with your partner photographer on these pics. Win-win for both of you.

Barbershops!
Don't be afraid to leave a stack of marketing materials at these places. No offense, guys, but the ladies are usually the ones doing the planning. They'll pick up your brochures and coupons and put them in their hefty wedding binder or hand them to their future groom at dinner.

TIP 38

Partner with a Jeweler

This one may not be as easy, particularly in the case of larger jewelry stores, but local jewelers may be open to a partnership, especially if you introduce yourself by dropping off some coffee and donuts. But, really, as a stylist or barber with people from all walks of life sitting in your chair, you hear all the juicy stuff—the engagements, the upcoming weddings. You could certainly mention the local jeweler and even have cards on hand should the client express interest. And the local jeweler could do the same, having your business cards and menus on hand. You could even suggest doing the hair and makeup for any marketing materials, with credit to your salon/spa/barbershop, of course.

Fun Idea!
If you're a manicurist, why not suggest a jewelry fashion show as a partner activity? How fun is this idea? You could have hand models come in showing off all the gorgeous, different nail styles that would showcase the jeweler's rings—and have some photos taken and displayed at the jeweler and at your salon or spa.

Barbershops
The men are typically the ones doing the asking and the ring shopping, so don't pass over this tip!

TIP 39

Partner with Catering Companies, Bakeries, or Cake Designers

Get to know your local catering companies—many of them cater to weddings in addition to business luncheons and other events, opening the door to plenty of new business for your salon/spa/barbershop and staff. Offer some free services to their employees so they get to know your salon/spa/barbershop. Work out a referral program. Use their services for events. Get them to put your menu in their brochures. When special occasions come up, you never know who may be calling you to make them look beautiful or handsome.

Find a bakery that specializes in wedding cakes, and develop a relationship to refer clients to each other. Offer some free services to staff so they get to know your salon. Work out a referral program. Get them to put your salon's menu in their brochures. Have them provide food samples for salon events—a tasteful way to spread the word.

TIP 40

Partner with Wedding Venues

Get to know the popular wedding venues in your community.

These can include:
- Country clubs
- Banquet halls in restaurants and churches
- Hotel ballrooms
- Community gardens
- Vineyards
- Museums
- Riverboats

These places also cater to other big events, such as business conferences, christenings, family parties, etc. So getting on their radar is a great thing!

As with catering companies, offer some free services to staff so they get to know your salon/spa/barbershop. Work out a referral program. Get them to put your menu in their brochures. Offer to do the hair and makeup for their advertising pieces (brochures, website) with credit and salon/spa/barbershop information listed, of course.

TIP 41

Partner with a Limo Company

Stretch limos are used almost exclusively for special events: weddings, proms, galas, fundraisers, etc. Women always want perfect hair on special event days, and men will likely book the limo. This makes a good basis to provide referrals for each other's businesses, sharing deals via social media and partner pages. Drop off some menus at their physical location. Also suggest doing the hair, grooming, and makeup for their advertising pieces with credit and salon/spa/barbershop information listed.

TIP 42

Partner with a Florist

Similarly, find a florist that's known for their wedding arrangements. Both florists and bakeries/cake designers know months in advance about upcoming weddings and can give you a solid referral if you have a relationship. At the same time, you may be one of the first to know when one of your customers gets engaged—so you can refer him or her to the bakery and florist. Get your salon's fresh flowers from your partner florist. And if a bride wants fresh flowers woven into her hair, use the florist's, and give credit to the business when posting the pics. Similarly, offer to do the hair for the florist's marketing materials with credit to the salon and stylist, of course.

Get The Word Out
Having a small tabletop sign made is invaluable. They're cheap and effective.

FUN IDEAS FOR WEDDING PARTNERSHIPS

TIP 43

Sponsor a Free Wedding

Offer free wedding services for a deserving couple—a military couple, for example. If you can collaborate with your wedding partners and get them to also provide a free dress, catering, photos, cake, flowers, etc., not only will you be helping a deserving couple but you will also be participating in a great human-interest story. People love to hear stories like these. Get the local newspaper, magazines, and news stations involved, and have them do a story on the free wedding. This should give your salon/spa/barbershop great exposure and generate a ton of new prospects.

TIP 44

The Wedding Industry

"I hope that when I'm eighty years old, people will still be talking about my wedding."
—Jennifer Hudson

As much as any other single event, a wedding is a day of beauty, that's why it makes sense to partner with everyone from wedding planners to florists to photographers. There's huge potential working with a wedding party, from getting the bride ready for her announcement/engagement photos to beautifying the bride, bridesmaids, mother of the bride, mother of the groom, and flower girl the day of the wedding. You can provide on-site service if the venue has space, or you can reserve your whole salon for the wedding party. Give the bride what she wants, and you'll become the go-to bridal stylist.

The Guys!
Don't forget the groom! He wants to look good too on this special day—and he's already spent a lot of money, what's a little more? Then there's the groomsmen, father of the bride, father of the groom, and ushers. Everyone's going to want a fresh haircut, shave, or beard trim. Heck, even the most macho guy may consent to other services as well for his wedding—from a nail file and trim (does he really want dirt under his fingernails for the ring photos?) to a facial and massage.

By forming partnerships with others in the wedding industry, you'll have a lot of people who are constantly in contact with brides and grooms recommending your services, and you can do the same for them.

With all these partners, make sure you do something for them, whether that's listing their service on your website under a partner page, keeping their business cards and brochures in your salon, or whatever ideas the two of you come up with.

Draw Wedding Business with Your Website

- **Have a page on your website dedicated to "Weddings" or "Bridal Party Services" or—especially if you're a barbershop—"Grooms."** Brides searching for salons in the area will want to quickly know your prices and policies.

- **Be the first in town to have a "Grooms" section on your website.** Become known as THE place to go for one-stop grooming for the groom and his groomsmen, providing haircuts, styles, and shaves, even nail trims and massages. Throw in some package deals.

- **Include a digital wedding lookbook.** It's really important to build a portfolio of your work to show to brides, grooms, and potential partners. No bride is going to leave the day to chance, and no partners are going to recommend you if they've never seen your work.

- **Include wedding partner businesses on a special "Partners" page.** Simple things like this go a long way.

Remember!
When working with brides, make sure you leave enough time to special order accessories and to practice unfamiliar or tricky styles.

Weddings
Time and Money
Potential Investments

Time

- Time it takes to create a web page and marketing materials announcing your work with weddings
- Time it takes to make a list of potential partners and research them
- Time it takes to reach out to these folks
- Time invested in promoting your partner business
- Time to plan events and promotions with your partners
- Time to put together a digital portfolio of your work to show potential partners and brides/grooms
- Time to follow up with potential customers gained through your partnerships
- Trial appointments for brides and bridal party
- Extra time to special order accessories and to learn more difficult styles
- Time to attend events to keep you in touch with wedding trends and styles

Money

- Cost of adding a page to your website showcasing your work with weddings and partnerships
- Cost of related marketing materials (like your tabletop sign)
- Subscription to papers or magazines that keep you in touch with local

businesses and events, such as bridal shows
- Cost to attend bridal shows
- Money for treating potential partners to coffee or a meal
- Cost of items to promote the partnership (e.g., keeping a bouquet of a partner florist's flowers in the salon)—these can often be bartered
- Stamps and postage for introduction letters and thank you cards (Don't forget thank you notes.)
- Marketing materials to leave at partner business
- Cost of discounted or free services
- Any referral fees/cut of the proceeds you give to your partner
- Related costs for planning an event or promotion with your partners

TRADE SHOWS AND COMMUNITY EVENTS

"Business leaders cannot be bystanders."
—Howard Schultz

Trade shows, expos, fairs, and exhibitions gather a whole bunch of people in common industries, interests, or demographics under one roof. There are beauty expos, bridal shows, craft shows, women's business expos—the list goes on and on. These are like the singles cruises of dating—you can reach a whole group of potential customers and partners at one time and in one swoop.

Why attend or participate in a trade show or community event?

- To reach a group of target clients
- To introduce yourself to potential partners (this is especially important with events like the bridal expo)
- To gain insider industry knowledge and skills that give you an edge over the competition

Attending or exhibiting at a trade show can vary wildly in price, from very inexpensive weekend-long events to pricey weeklong affairs; check with show organizers on exhibition costs and requirements, and check the trade show website for registration fees. Participation may range from having a booth at the show to attending the show and sharing your information with exhibitors there. You can also provide a prize—perhaps a free service or a gift basket with your retail products—for the raffles held so often at exhibits or trade shows. And have some goodies on the table with your salon/spa/barbershop's name and information.

Are Trade Shows Worth It?

"One of the main benefits of appearing at a trade show over selling to individuals is that it's just like running a retail store. People are coming in the door to talk to you. What you should be looking at is the value of a sale. You can look at it as the value of a single sale, or as the lifetime value of a client. If selling to one or two or three people will pay for a trade show, it's a good place for you to be."
—Linda Bishop, founder of sales training and marketing consulting firm Thought Transformation [1]

Many of the people attending a local trade show may have never heard of you or the salon/spa/barbershop you own or work in. That alone makes trade shows worth the time and money. Letting people know who you are, what you do, and where they can find you is good business and time well spent.

Of course, the fact that trade shows offer a lot of chances for boosting business doesn't guarantee success. To maximize the value of a trade show appearance, it's important to find the events that are best suited to promoting your salon, barbershop, nail salon, or spa and making an impact on the market.

How to find local trade shows:

- Your city's convention center
- Local chamber of commerce
- Local business magazines, newspapers, and websites
- Small business development centers
- Your product vendors

How do you get people in your booth? Show them what you do. Get a model and put makeup on her. Cut some hair. Be dynamic.

Six Tips for Rocking a Trade Show

1. Consider what clients you are trying to reach or partnerships you are trying to make, then find trade shows that cater to them.

2. Prepare before the event; know who will be there. Make a list of booths you will visit, for example.

3. Use Forbes.com contributor Ken Krogue's business card trick: Keep your business cards in your right pocket and other peoples' in your left. Before you put another's card in your pocket, jot some notes down on the card so you can remember the individual or business to personalize the follow-up. (Trust me, this is true!)

4. If you have two people, have one of you near the booth and the other a bit further away, encouraging others (in a nonpushy way) to visit the booth. Don't bullhorn people as they pass.

5. Follow up. Research from InsideSales.com has shown that sales folks should follow up six to nine times. [2]

6. Be sure you get an exhibitors list. These lists often have contact information on them, so they're invaluable for follow up calls or emails.

If you have a booth at a trade show, the most important thing is to collect information from potential clients. Having a raffle is a great way to do this. Have a space on the back of entry forms for entrants to put their name, email, phone, and birthday (and wedding date if it's a bridal event). And, of course, follow up with these individuals. Send an email with a discounted or free quickie service, and also blast an email at their birthday with the same.

Trade Shows and Community Events
Time and Money
Potential Investments

Time

- Time to find a trade show or community event to participate in
- Time to plan your booth and any related workshops/demos/presentations
- Time to compile marketing materials
- Time to put together a digital portfolio of your work to show attendees
- Time to attend the event
- Time to follow up with contacts

Money

- Cost of the trade show or event (admission attendance or booth rental) and related travel expenses
- Cost of promotional materials or freebies
- Cost of raffle items
- Subscription to papers or magazines that keep you in touch with shows and events
- Cost of discounted or free services
- Cost of membership to organizations that put on events
- Related costs for planning an event of your own (cost of venue, marketing materials, food, decorations, donations, etc.) (See the *Implementation Guide* at the end of the book for a more detailed idea of the budget involved in planning a successful event.)

Time and Money
Trade show success is based on how much time you want to spend and how much time you want to invest. Spend the time planning for and really working a show, and it's worth it; spend the money on the best shows and you'll see a great return.

TIP 45

Wedding/Bridal Shows and Expos

Every bride wants to look beautiful on her wedding day, so every bride and even the bridesmaids, mother of the bride, mother of the groom, and rest of the wedding party are all potential customers. If you're trying to get new customers, a great way to meet individuals and the whole family at once is to exhibit at wedding shows. If you've done other weddings, include large photo displays or an album or digital montage of those to show off your experience. For an extra punch, you can have some bridal party models in your booth. Make sure you set up an iPad to collect information for your database. Keep it simple: collect a name, email address, telephone number, and wedding date. Asking for a birth date can also be effective as you can send out a birthday email as well, providing a discount or free service that lures in the client. Collecting data is critical in today's fast-moving world.

TIP 46

Maternity/Baby Expos

New moms need all the pampering they can get, which means maternity or baby expos are the perfect place to find new clients. Get a booth at a baby expo, gather information including due dates, and send new moms a gift certificate. Can you imagine the goodwill and positive word of mouth this will cause? *Suzie's Salon gave me a free service when I had my baby...* Let your salon be a welcoming place for new moms.

For events where babies and toddlers are present, offer a keepsake package so the mothers can keep that first lock of hair. And don't forget some wine to offer mommy.

TIP 47

Fashion Shows

Participating in a local fashion show is a great way to promote your business. Too, they're often done as part of a charity event in which case you're supporting a good cause at the same time.

Offer to do the hair and makeup for the show in trade for credit in the brochures and advertisements. The announcer should also give you credit during the show. If you get involved early enough, you may be able to arrange a special hair segment or makeup moment based on the time of the year, season, and theme of the event. What a great way to not only promote your talents but also show that you're capable of formulating *any* look on *any* one who walks through the door of your salon/spa/barbershop.

Hey Dudes!
Hey dudes (barbers), keep in mind that guys also walk the runways at these happenings. What a great way to promote your mad barbering skills and to show off your talent.

You may also be able to get some publicity in the media promoting the events—maybe some hair, grooming, or makeup Q&As with pics and contact information.

TIP 48

Home and Garden Shows

Women between the ages of 30 and 50 are the prime attendees for these shows, which is an excellent target market for new clients. If you have booth space, consider having a hair show or cutting and styling in the booth to attract attention. If you do makeup or nails, do some makeovers and manicures. If it's a flower show, incorporate some of the local buds in the hairstyles. If it's a home show, try to partner with a few of the local businesses to take some pics of impeccably styled models to go along with the products and services—a model getting ready in front of a beautiful bathroom sink, for example.

Make sure you collect attendee information during the show and follow up with them once you're back in the salon.

TIP 49

Sponsor an Event

Think about being a sponsor for an event. Not only are you promoting community goodwill but you are also getting advertising in the process. Depending on the event, you may get various levels of advertising based on how much you contribute. Do a little research.

Sponsoring events can be quite costly, so keep in mind there are different ways to become a sponsor, from offering services, offering your salon space, or offering up your time. You can also pay to become a sponsor. When you do your research, decide where you'll get the most bang for your buck.

TIP 50

Other Fairs and Festivals

These events bring many women from the local community, making them an ideal place to meet potential new customers. Consider renting a booth and teaching some cool hairdos or makeup techniques—especially those that apply to the event. If it's a folk festival, share some cool braiding techniques, for example.

Remember to collect information and follow up.

Shaking hands with and introducing yourself to other booth holders may also yield some results. Networking with other creative businesspeople is always a good thing.

Events like this are your chance to get weird, get wild, get funky. Do something that will make you get noticed (in a good way) and promote your business and creative skills.

TIP 51

Beer Fests

Beer fests attract men of all ages (and ladies, too) but especially men in their twenties and thirties. Craft beer and pubs that serve it are on trend these days—along with beards and guys caring more about their appearance. Get in on it. Consider sponsoring the event and getting some publicity, or even have a booth. Call it "Beards and Brews" or something like that. Have people vote on the best beard, weirdest beard, most creative beard, etc. You could build buzz by having people vote beforehand, or you could have some models available or big blown-up pics to vote on—they could even be of current customers, which is a win-win as it shows your mad skills while also promoting customer retention and goodwill. You know they'll be bragging on it to their friends and sharing via social media. Have fun with this. On the back of the voting slips, make sure to include space for customer info: name, email, phone, and birthday for birthday freebies. On the table, give away coupons for discount haircuts, a free trim or shave for first-time customers, etc.; promotional items (e.g., a beer cozy or comb with your barbershop's name on it); and munchies.

While at the event, connect with some local craft brewers.

TIP 52

Business Networking Events

Getting involved with local business groups and attending meetings and events is an excellent way to build your client base—you might even become the token professional beauty advice columnist for the group's newsletters and social media, building your name that way. Every businessperson needs to look his or her best to maintain a professional reputation.

Also consider the larger events sponsored by these groups and how you can get involved—whether with a sponsorship (and advertising for you.), a booth, on-site professional makeovers, a hair and makeup fashion show or advice segment, etc.

You could also put on an event for these organizations—think professional hairdos, grooming for the professional, makeup looks for great first impressions. You could have so much fun with this. All businesspeople want to look polished, and you have just the skills to help them look their best. You could also get some of your partners involved.

At most of these functions, people are standing with a cocktail or snack in hand, so a great way to get the attention of the crowd is to march models through showing off that awesome cut or style. Most people are there for the drinks, food, and friends, so you have small window to grab their attention.

TIP 53

Car and Boat Shows

"There's three things men always talk about—women, sports, and cars."
—Mario Lopez

Classic car shows and boat shows attract certain kinds of men—those with money and those who care about looking good. Why not take advantage of that and be a sponsor for the shows or have a booth at one of these events? Partner with a photographer and have him or her take pics of your clients with classic cars—your clients will tell all their friends about it. Man a booth together and sell the pics (have your barbershop's or salon's business card tucked into the corner and credited on the back). Booths for these shows usually run about $50–$75. Have business cards, coupons, menus, combs with your imprinted barbershop or salon name, vendor samples stickered with your business name on them, etc. on the table. There's a lot you could do with this. What about quick how-to demonstrations of the cool "greased" hair looks of the 50s, for example? Classic cars—anything retro or vintage—are cool these days; these shows aren't just for the older gents.

You could also sponsor the event and gain some publicity for your barbershop/salon/spa.

PART 2

Attract Clients like Bees to Honey

SOCIAL MEDIA

A 2013 Nielsen study found American adults, on average, spend 11 hours a day with electronic media. [1]

How much time did you spend on your smartphone or computer today? How many minutes (or hours) did you spend on Facebook? Checking email? Posting on Instagram? Watching pet videos on YouTube?

Having an online presence is essential. And most social media tools are free and easy to learn and put you in touch with huge numbers of potential clients.

If we're not taking advantage of social media to attract clients, we're just being stupid. Even if you're a technophobe, there are tons of instructional videos and help out there as well as tech-savvy people in your salon and inner circles to help you. Heck, ask a 5-year-old; they probably know more about tech than you do (no judgment here—this applies to us, too).

Promote Yourself!
If your salon is not on board with social media, get on the boat! Volunteer to set up a Facebook page or Instagram account. And don't wait to set up your own page promoting yourself; there's no one saying you can't set up a profile on Facebook or **Bloom.com** to display pictures of your work and get the word out. Be sure to check out **StyleNet.com** while you're at it.

While we can't guarantee these social media platforms will still be around by the time this book reaches your hands (technology changes every single day), this section presents the social media that have been going strong with no signs of losing steam.

Most of these tips don't cost anything yet yield huge results. *Free*, we emphasize, *free*.

You have to find a balance between being online too much and not being on there at all, but YOU MUST BE ONLINE. It's essential for people to be able to find you online. You have to announce sales and specials, show photos of current trends and hairstyles, and be active with your customers. The minute you aren't active, someone else is there filling your space.

If you're not taking advantage of social media, you're missing out.

Link Your Social Media Platforms
What's super cool about these social media platforms is they can almost all be linked together—meaning if you write a Twitter post, it can go to Facebook and Google+, and vice versa. You can even write postings ahead of time and schedule them to post on a certain date and time. This means keeping your social media fresh is so much easier. Check out services like **Hootsuite** and **TweetDeck**; each has free versions.

Social Media Time and Money
Potential Investments

Time
- Time to set up each social media platform
- Time to set up a digital portfolio of your work
- Time to plan, shoot, and edit instructional videos
- Time each day to update social media
- Time to follow and promote partner businesses (as they should be doing for you as well)

Money
- Smartphone or a good digital camera to take pics
- Video camera for short, instructional videos
- Videographer
- Web designer
- Web content writer
- Domain name (www.salonname.com)
- Web hosting services
- Online ads
- Photo and video editing software
- Fees for online platforms to showcase your work

TIP 54

Create or Revamp Your Website

"97 percent of consumers search online for products and services —yet 58 percent of small businesses do not have a website (Google, 2012)." [1]

The first order of business in successfully using the web to your advantage is having a top-notch website. If you don't already have a website, get on board and create one today. Even if you were ahead of the game and have had a website for decades (*especially* if you've had a website for decades), it may be time to revamp it. If people come across your business name, either through your successful advertising, word of mouth, or just by accident, their next step will most likely be pulling out the smartphone and checking you out on the web. If you have a lackluster website or one not optimized for mobile phones (we'll discuss this later), this will impact their impression of you and, fairly or not, the services you provide. Make sure your site is professional, stylish, and informative.

Don't Rely on Your Facebook Page
While some businesses today use their Facebook pages as their primary site, we still recommend having an old-fashioned website independent of a social media channel like Facebook. Some people don't belong to Facebook, and with an independent website, your content and design are under **your** control (no hair-pulling frustration when Facebook updates its system yet again).

What to Include on Your Website

So what should you include on your website? Here's a handy little checklist to get you started.

√ **Salon contact information**: name, location, phone number, email address, addresses of other social media.

TIP: A picture of the outside of your salon may help a new customer to find it more easily.

√ **Salon hours**

√ **Menu of services** with prices

√ **Specials** (make sure these are updated and current)

√ **Appealing images** of the salon, maybe stylists in action, and some of your great end products—make sure to get permission for any customer pictures you post

Technophobes!

If you're a technophobe and the thought of creating a website sends you into a panic, see if this is a task another salon worker will embrace, maybe your front-desk person. There are also many companies that will create a website for you, including ones tailored to the beauty industry, such as **StyleNet**. These range from companies that create the site and turn it over to you to maintain to companies that will create and then manage your site for you. Just remember that your site will be constantly evolving, so the ability to make timely changes via you or your web person is essential.

Do-It-Yourselfers

If you decide to build your own website, you will need to purchase a domain name (www.salonname.com) and choose a web host service, such as GoDaddy—basically, you're renting space on the Internet just as you would rent a building on a street. Most of these web hosts offer website-building programs, some at a fee. Most offer free tutorials. There are tons of books and online tools to help you.

Costs can vary depending on whether your site is done in-house or whether you pay an outside company to build your site. Although you will have to pay a couple hundred to a couple thousand dollars if someone else creates your site, do it if necessary—having a great web presence is a must in today's environment.

Proofread!
Make sure the information on your site isn't riddled with errors. Have an editor friend give it a read through; glaring typos look unprofessional.

What Is SEO? How Important Is It?

When someone types your business's name into a search engine, it's important that it shows up on the first few pages. **SEO** stands for **search engine optimization,** and learning some of the tricks of SEO (or hiring an expert if you have the funds to do so) can help your page rank higher when individuals search your salon by name or even make a general search for salons in their geographic area. Can you imagine the potential customers—all the new people moving into an area and searching for a salon and finding yours first?

SEO tricks involve adding keywords, coding language, etc. If you're the salon popping up on a search engine's first page (and your site looks good), you've probably landed a new customer. Convenience is a key asset.

"Smartphones and social media expand our universe. We can connect with others or collect information easier and faster than ever."
—Daniel Goleman

TIP 55

It's a MUST to Make Your Site Mobile-Friendly

A 2013 study by the Android app Locket showed the average smartphone user checks their phone 110 times a day; another by Kleiner Perkins Caufield and Byers found 150 to be more accurate. [1]

Everyone has a smartphone these days, and we use them for everything: to make calls, to find the nearest restaurant, to see whether a store is open, to look for a phone number, to find coupons while out shopping. And if your website is not mobile-friendly, Google looks unfavorably on it, and it won't show up high in the search rankings—READ: people won't be able to find you. If your website is not mobile-friendly, then you're at a serious disadvantage.

Check Your Site
Google has a Mobile-Friendly Test tool that lets you plug in your web address for a quick test: **https://www.google.com/webmasters/tools/mobile-friendly/**. You should also look at how your site looks on a number of devices: iPhone, Android, tablets, etc.

We don't want to get too techy here, but to make your website mobile-friendly, the buzzword is *responsive design*; this means your website will automatically adjust depending on the device. And, if you do nothing else, you can make your site more mobile-friendly by making your design simpler, having readable fonts, and putting critical information (name of the salon, phone number, address) at the top left.

TIP 56

Text-Message Marketing

Since people are so attached to their phones, why not take advantage of this with *text-message marketing*, sometimes called *SMS* (short message service) *marketing*? When clients sign up, they'll receive special coupons and the latest news about salon/spa/barbershop promotions, specials, and events.

Why is text-message marketing such a great idea? Well, not only do people's phones ding every time they receive a text message, they'll more likely read your text messages because they're short and, most importantly, they've signed up for them. They're invested and want to receive the messages.

Moneywise, this form of marketing is pretty cheap, just a few cents per message, or you could go with the flat-rate package deals. There are tons of services out there that will guide you through the setup and help you track results.

TIP 57

Offer E-gifts

Give people the option to purchase e-gifts on your website. This adds another layer of customers and income base—out-of-towners. Friends, family, and businesspersons wanting to send a gift to a client can simply hop onto the website and—voilà!—quick-and-easy present. Promote this service heavily around holidays—especially the big ones like Christmas, Mother's Day, and Father's Day. Or what about Teacher Appreciation or Administrative Professionals Week?

TIP 58

Facebook

"Think about what people are doing on Facebook today. They're keeping up with their friends and family, but they're also building an image and identity for themselves, which in a sense is their brand. They're connecting with the audience that they want to connect to. It's almost a disadvantage if you're not on it now."
—Mark Zuckerberg

Since everyone uses Facebook, it's an excellent way to reach a huge number of clients and potential clients. Think about it, every time your current clients like your salon's or stylist's page or share something from it, you're reaching all their friends, which can be hundreds to thousands per client.

First things first, you'll want to create a Facebook *business* page. Facebook provides tutorials on how to get started setting up your page. It's quite simple.

Partnerships
Having a Facebook business page is a great way for you and your business partners to promote each other's businesses and reach even more clients. "Like" their pages and share posts from their page; encourage them to do the same for you.

So what can you put on this business page? Tons. Think contact information, special promotions, beauty/grooming tips and videos, and pictures of your cuts, colors, and styles or the ones you see that are inspiring. And unlike a website, which can be more time-consuming or expensive to update on a daily basis, your Facebook page can be updated in real time. (**Note:** It's still important to have a primary website and to keep it current with prices, fresh pics, and specials. Not everyone uses Facebook, and your website will likely be the first item people find when they search for you.)

What to Include on Your Facebook Business Page

Cover Photo
Choosing a picture of the outside of your salon/spa/barbershop for the page's cover photo may help a new customer to find your business more easily.

About
Include the following in the "About" section:
- √ Contact information (name, location, phone number, email address)
- √ Hours
- √ Website address
- √ Short description of the salon/spa/barbershop
- √ Awards won
- √ Product lines

Photos
- √ Include pictures of your stylists' or barbers' handiwork: kick-ass haircuts, shaves, styles, makeovers, nail design, etc. (Important: Be sure to ask for permission before posting customer photos.)

Picture Albums
You can put these pictures into albums for specific things: Wedding Styles, Nail Art, Guy Styles, Shaves, etc. to make it easier for customers. You can even choose the cover image for each album.

Reviews

Glowing customer reviews (real people!) can do wonders to send more people toward your salon/spa/barbershop. Haven't you ever read customer reviews on a product to see how real people liked it?

Negative Reviews
Be sure to respond quickly to negative reviews. Negative word of mouth spreads fast. **IMPORTANT:** Never attack the negative review. Offer a service to correct it, invite the person back, and smother him or her with kindness. Don't put out fire with fire. Remember, the customer is always right.

Timeline

Include the following on your timeline:

√ Daily and weekly specials

√ Fresh pics (which will automatically be added to the "Photos" page of the site)

√ Fun beauty or grooming tips

√ Links to a beauty blog

√ Links to instructional beauty or grooming videos (these are automatically posted to the "Videos" page)

Have a Contest!
To gain more Facebook likes and to have your content shared, you can host a contest in which people share your post for a chance to win a free service or product. If you do this on a regular basis, people will visit your page just to enter and share. Think of the free publicity!

Videos

Post links to instructional beauty or grooming videos—even better if they're from your own stylists/barbers.

Events

You can post salon/spa/barbershop events using this feature.

Adding regular, useful content to your Facebook page, such as beauty tips, links to instructional videos, and links to your blog or other noncompetitors' blogs or videos, ups your site views and leads to more regular visitors. People will visit to see what tips you've posted and what sales/promotions are running.

Have your front-desk person devote a portion of each day to updating the page.

Facebook Ads
Facebook ads are another way to get your business in the eyes of more people. You can target your ads to reach particular audiences and set a budget.

Salon Owners
Have your stylists, nail techs, and front desk employees post to your page or at least tag the salon in their post. This is a great way to easily market a new stylist, or product. Tag everything and everyone you can, from the products to the salon to the stylist to the client, and in many cases, you'll get a response or repost from some of the top industry product manufacturers giving you a shout out on Facebook. How's that for reaching a big audience?

TIP 59

Digital Lookbooks and Online Portfolios

Ever notice how many customers look through hairstyle books while they're sitting in your waiting area or under a dryer? Create the digital version by taking pictures of some of your best work and posting groups of these pictures on your website, Facebook business page, and on a site like Bloom.com, formatting them similarly to the traditional stylebooks. Include popular, current styles; great colors; and some hip, trendy styles. In addition to showing off what your stylists are capable of, these pics flatter the customers you ask to photograph and use on your site. Not only will they go check out their picture online, they'll send the link to all their friends! Most of your clients will be flattered if you want to use their picture to show off your latest creation.

Stylists
Sites like **Bloom.com** are a great way to display your talents and gain attention! Basically, this is like Facebook for stylists! You can post your photos and videos and create digital lookbooks. You can also share these photos to your other social media like Twitter and Facebook. You can gain followers and even book clients from the site.

Just Post Some Pictures Already!
Even just posting pics on your Facebook page in an album is something.

TIP 60

Google+ and Google My Business

What *is* Google+? Well, it's a social networking site, similar in some ways to Facebook. There's a wall where you can post shareable content such as status updates and pictures and videos (pictures and videos are automatically categorized on the "Photos" and "Videos" pages as well). Instead of "liking" a post, you click the "+1" button. You can even allow people to post reviews (again, remember to respond to negative views quickly, showing future customers that you care about getting things right).

In your "About" page, you can put all your salon/spa/barbershop contact information, including the website address of your business. You can even include a short description of the salon/spa/barbershop and a tag line. And, just like Facebook, you can choose a "profile" pic and a cover image (suggestions are pictures of your storefront, your logo, a striking beauty image, etc.).

When you have a Gmail address, you automatically receive a Google+ account. This means that you can create a Google My Business page.

Google My Business is the *business version* of Google+, and it has the same benefits but is even better because your business can be found in Google Search, Maps, and Google+. Follow the prompts on https://www.google.com/business/ to get started.

Simply having a Google+ account puts you higher in Google's search rankings, and most people still use Google as their primary search engine. What makes Google My Business pages awesome is that when someone searches you on Google, your business profile and related pics pop up—LARGE—on the right-hand side of the screen along with your business's address and a Google Maps image of its location.

Stylists and Barbers!
You should still sign up for a Gmail address and Google+ account. It's a great way to promote yourself! Read on!

Five Ways to Find Followers

Just as with Twitter and Facebook, you'll want to gather some **followers** so your information pops up on their pages. Here are five ways to find them.

1. Go to the "People" link in the left drop-down menu of your profile page. There are tons of ways to find people to follow (your email contacts, etc.). Follow these folks, and they'll likely follow back.

2. Add a Google+ badge (icon) to your website so visitors can quickly add you to their Google+ circles (a.k.a. "Follow" you).

3. Include your Google+ name on all marketing materials, and encourage customers and friends and family to follow you.

4. If you have partner businesses (a gym, dance studio, etc.), follow them, include their links on your "About" page, and also share their specials on your page. When they do the same, you are reaching an even broader audience.

5. Share good content, and it will get shared and reach more people.

Poll Fun!
Google+ even has a fun, easy poll feature in which you pose questions to your followers and they vote. Imagine the fun possibilities. You can have your followers vote on celebrity hairstyles, nail colors to purchase for the salon, etc. How about letting your customers into the decision-making process? What special do they like better? What hairstyles do they want to see featured for a discount? What nail polish brand should we carry: OPI or __? Let them feel their opinion matters.

TIP 61

Twitter

Twitter has become one of the top social media platforms, comparable to Facebook. You set up a profile, follow people, and post to your wall. The only difference is your wall messages (tweets) can only be 140 characters, and anyone can follow you.

You can tweet Twitter-only special offers such as sales on retail items or discounts on services. You can also announce current promotions and your participation in any community or charity events. You can even tweet hair-care tips or links to instructional videos or blog posts. It's all about engaging your customers. The more useful content you post and the more regularly you post it, the more people will keep tabs on your page. And the more often you'll show up in their feeds.

> **Post Useful Content**
> When your followers retweet (share) your tweet (post), it shows up on their followers' newsfeeds (more potential customers!). So the more useful the content, the more likely people are to share.

Hashtags (keywords or key phrases used after a pound # sign) are what Twitter is known for. They can be a useful tool for being found and noticed by a great number of people. People can search for a particular hashtag topic in Twitter's search box. Consider not only adding keyword or key-phrase hashtags such as #weddinghair or #nailart but also *location-specific hashtags* such as #salonlocation and #salonlocationpluskeyword—for example, #denver and #denverhairsalons. If targeting a particular audience, say brides, add a hashtag such as #denverbrides.

Link to Facebook
You can even link your Tweets to Facebook so they post there as well.

Ask your current customers and followers on other social media to follow you or your business on Twitter, and then build from there. The more Twitter followers you have, the more potential customers you'll reach.

Follow Local Businesses and Partners for More Followers
Following local businesses ups your chances of them following you back, leading to your salon/spa/barbershop being in the sight of a greater local audience. Also follow your partners' pages, and retweet each other's specials and posts.

It takes barely any time at all to set up a Twitter account for yourself or your salon. Daily, regular posting is key. Maybe have your front-desk person update the site as one of his or her daily tasks.

TIP 62

Instructional Videos (YouTube, Vine, Instagram)

Think about how many pet videos you watched this week. C'mon, don't be afraid to admit it. it, we all fall for our four-legged friends, and we all share those videos on Facebook or show them on our phones. Short videos are hot.

So think how having short, instructional videos on hair, shaves, trims, makeup, nails, etc. could up the publicity for your salon or barbershop. These videos are easy to share and make you current. Plus, your mad skills are right out there for the whole world to see. For the dudes out there with crazy skills in barbering, don't be shy with YouTube when it comes to showing off your latest and greatest fades or beard trims.

These videos can be shared with/posted on your other social media channels as well.

The Top Dogs: YouTube, Vine, and Instagram

YouTube, owned by Google, is still number one in video watchers and subscribers, and these videos can be of any length and are easily shareable. **Vines** are six seconds; **Instagram** videos can be up to fifteen seconds. (Instagram is known more for its photo sharing, but its videos are gaining in popularity.)

YouTube is a great place to create a video channel where you can post longer-form how-to videos of hairstyles, etc. But today, with people's limited attention spans, Vines and Instagram videos can be great, too. You can take a hint from companies like Lowes with their "Fix in Six" videos on Vine in which the company presents a quick six-second how-to. Remember to hashtag your videos, just as you do with Twitter or Google+.

Your channel names for these services can be your salon/spa/barbershop's name. You can also include pics of your salon/spa/barbershop and its logo as well as a brief description. Remember to watermark all photos with your business name.

It only takes a few minutes to set up a video account. However, shooting these videos can take as long or as little as you want. With the video recording on phones these days, it wouldn't be hard to record short videos. Smartphones have video-recording features of decent quality, but you may want to use better equipment for long-form YouTube videos. You may choose to have a friend record these short videos and do the editing, or you could choose to hire someone, but keep in mind, a videographer could cost a couple hundred dollars.

Remember to attract the 18 to 29 crowd on Instagram and Tumblr. It's the best way to connect is with new and edgy cuts and styles. Stay on top of fashion trends that are happening today. All of your younger clients use Instagram.

TIP 63

Start a Beauty or Grooming Blog

Everyone has a favorite blog. (In case you need a refresher, a *blog* is an online magazine or journal of sorts that allows you to post articles, quotes, etc.) There are tons of popular beauty blogs; make yours one of them!

Readers can subscribe to your blog and even share posts with their friends on social media, which means their contacts learn about your salon/spa/barbershop too.

Five Great Ideas for Blog Topics

1. Product Reviews
2. Events
3. Before and After
4. Salon and Staff News
5. Tips and Trends [1]

It doesn't take a lot of time to set up a blog. And there are plenty of free blogging services—two of the most popular include WordPress and Blogger. Try to be consistent with posting—especially good is scheduling your posts to go out at certain times so that people start to expect them. You'll also want to spend time each day responding to comments. Think of it as good customer service.

TIP 64

Digital/E-newsletters

Create a digital newsletter to send to your customers. Most important is that you include useful content and exclusive deals that make them click "open" and not "delete."

Some ideas:

- Include easy how-to's, such as how to use a certain hair product you sell to get the hottest beachy look for summer.
- Show off a new makeup color in a series of photos.
- Include newsletter-exclusive deals.
- Profile a stylist or barber.
- Include upcoming salon events and promotions.

Attention! Attention!
Remember the importance of a strong email **subject line**. Think of this like a magazine headline that catches your eye in the checkout aisle; these must grab the reader's instant attention.

TIP 65

Create How-To Stories on Snapchat & Periscope

Snapchat is the newest "It Girl" of social media. And no wonder: the median age of those who use the platform is 17. Snapchat is rending over 10 billion views per day, according to recent reports. Snapchat rivals Facebook's reach. Allow your Snaps to serve as inspiration to those who may want the services you provide. Snapchat and Periscope are great for showing off before and after shots of your clients, friends and family. Use these platforms for tutorials and how to create your styles at home once your clients leave the salon. It's also a great way to keep clients involved with your life when your not working in the salon.

TIP 66

Check-In Apps: Yelp Can Help

Check-in apps are hot. They allow your customers to "check in" to your business and let their friends and followers know they're getting pampered, dolled up, and are doing it in style. When they "check in" they'll do it through Facebook, Yelp, or Foursquare (or all three). Once they do, they can post reviews and photos.

These check-ins are seen by all their friends, giving you free-and-easy publicity. One salon, The Root Salon in Phoenix, saw an increase of two dozen more clients a week when it had just a dozen reviews on Yelp; when they did a $300 print ad for a month, they saw just one additional customer.[1] Now, with over a hundred reviews, we bet their chairs are always warm.

If you're the business owner, you can claim your business on these apps and respond to reviews, choose the highlighted photos, etc. With Foursquare, you can even send special deals to customers—for their first check-in, for example.

 **Yelp** can be the death of a company or stylists. If you get a good review, thank them. If you get a bad review, settle the issue politely and offer a free corrective service. Above all, do not argue your point, just smother them with kindness.

TIP 67

Groupon and LivingSocial: Daily Deal Sites

Everyone loves Groupon. Groupon subscribers get daily deals for local businesses at a discounted rate of 40–60 percent, and in order for the deal to be valid, it has to be *redeemed* (bought) by a certain number of people (this goal is set by the seller—you). This means that the Groupon user is encouraged to share the deal with others so it reaches its quota—more customers. If the deal doesn't reach its quota, no one owes anything.

While Groupon means you're offering heavily discounted services and paying a fee to Groupon if you reach your quota, this could be a great way to get an influx of new customers into your chair. And once they get there, we all know they'll come back.

Awesome Benefit!
Another benefit is that Groupon shares the email addresses of all those who purchased the daily deal, giving businesses an awesome resource to **follow up** with these new customers.

LivingSocial is a competitor of Groupon and offers similar benefits to subscribers. The cool thing about LivingSocial is that when a user shares a deal link and gets three other people to purchase the deal through the link, the original sharer gets the deal free.

Seal the Deal!

The people who use these sites are coming to you not because you're special or because they know you but because they see an unbelievable value for what you're offering. (It's all about the price with Groupon!) But daily deal sites are a great way to get people in the door, especially on slow days. The key is keeping these people and making them yours. So you've found a date; now how do you get to the second or third date? What do they say, once you get to the third date, you've **sealed the deal**?

TIP 68

Craigslist Ads: Free Advertising!

Post a free advert under the *Services* section of Craigslist. Spend time crafting a catchy "posting title." Advertise special deals and promos. In the "posting body," let people know what services you or your salon/spa/barbershop offers, any specialties, and the retail products carried. Put in your salon/spa/barbershop name, address, phone number, and hours of operation. Adding your address to the "show on maps" section allows you to add a map to your posting, which is extra helpful for customers.

Your Name Is Everything

It's important to keep tabs on your web reputation. Search your business on Google and see what comes up. Search your name, too. If you're the owner, encourage your employees to keep a professional web presence as well. They are representing the salon/spa/barbershop. Revealing, drunken photos, just NO.

We recommend that you designate someone in the shop to manage social media. Pay them extra, over, and above their salary or commission. This is the marketing future.

And follow the social media of successful salons, businesses, etc.—this is acceptable stalking. Get ideas.

TRADITIONAL ADVERTISING

"Many a small thing has been made large by the right kind of advertising."
—Mark Twain

Advertising is calling attention to your business by paying for announcements about your business in broadcast, print, or electronic media.

Traditional media like television, radio, newspapers, and magazines—unlike social media—doesn't talk back. The fact that your ad will remain what you intended is a plus for using the traditional advertising methods discussed in this section.

There are costs to traditional advertising, so it's important to know your target and to fit the medium with the audience. What magazines do they read? When are they listening to the radio? Which programs? What TV shows do they watch? Also, monitor how new customers heard of you; did your ad work?

*"It's hard to make money unless you spend money.
Good advertising dollars means profit at the end of the day."*
—Eric Ryant

Traditional Advertising Time and Money

Because each of these mediums has a cost, we include the investments of time and money with each tip.

Traditional Is Cool!
While some may say print is dead, the world's response to actor Benedict Cumberbatch's humble newspaper wedding announcement shows that sometimes going traditional, going against the grain, is cool and attention-getting in itself.

TIP 69

Television Ads

TV advertising can be expensive, but if it reaches a large amount of people in your target audience, it can be worth it. With TV, think more of programs your target audience watches rather than channels or networks. Also consider *what* you're sharing; amazing, limited-time specials and promos grab attention.

Cost

Local Television: Small companies that are looking at local television stations will find smaller costs for advertising. Rates for running the ad can vary from $200 to $1,500 for a thirty-second spot, according to Entrepreneur magazine, and most stations allow two minutes of local advertising each hour. Prices change depending on market size and competition, time of day aired, and how many times you choose to run the ad. The cost to produce (create the ad) ranges from $200 to $1,500 for a thirty-second commercial.[1] Some stations will produce your ad at no cost if you sign up for a certain number of television spots. Ask about this; don't be afraid to negotiate a bit.

 Be smart and know your target market—what days and times of day are they watching TV? What programs are they watching?

Time

This will take a full day if not two for a photo shoot and also the time it takes to come up with a concept and craft your message—to get down exactly what you want to say and show new and existing clients.

TIP 70

Radio Spots

The radio is still a hot medium. We listen to the radio while driving to and from work, at work, and at home most workplaces have a radio playing, so your message gets heard multiple times during the day.

You want to pick radio stations that your target audience is listening to. Think too of the pivotal drive times: when people are driving to and from work and the lunch hour.

When crafting your commercial, think about the message you are trying to convey to your target customers and what you want them to do. The key to the commercial is having a compelling call to action that drives your target customers to your business. Keep it simple and to the point.

Look into sponsoring weather or traffic reports as an inexpensive way to get your name out there.

Cost

So what does the radio commercial production process cost? Well, there are two main costs—the cost to produce the ad and the cost to air the ad. Sometimes, radio stations offer production services as well. Airtime is typically in time increments of 30, 60, or 120 seconds[1]. The price for a commercial with one voice ranges from about $300 to $500 per commercial. If you add another voice or jingle singers, you will pay more. Costs to air the ad for one week will typically range from $500 to a couple thousand, depending on whether you're in a smaller town or a larger metro area.[2]

Time

We suggest putting aside a full day to put together a two to three minute radio ad. You can save plenty of time and money by knowing what you would like to say in advance.

Charities and Benefits
Do a charity or benefit in your salon, and the radio station will probably give you free airtime to support the cause. It might just take a phone call. Most people are very giving when it comes to charity work (it does good for the radio's image, too, to be involved). Try a cut-a-thon for cancer.

TIP 71

Newspaper Ads

Some say print is dead, but newspapers still have a loyal following, especially among those thirty-five and up. Major cities have readerships over 100,000, and smaller cities in the tens of thousands.[1] Many still pick up the newspaper to check out weekend happenings and on Sundays to find coupon deals.

With newspaper advertising, you have a lot of control. Request that your ad run in the newspaper sections your target audience will read—barbershops, for example, might consider sports; salons, the lifestyle section. Think *special inserts* as well—weekend event inserts (great place to advertise date-night and going-out specials), holiday inserts (holiday promos and events), and local big-event inserts (build a promo around the community event—you could even be an event sponsor).

> **Add a Coupon!**
> Add a coupon to your ad. This way, you can track how successful the ad was by collecting these coupons.

Where should you place your newspaper ad? General consensus says the top half of a page (this is called "above the fold"), on the right-hand page, and next to an article. You don't want your ad to be swallowed up by a crowd of other ads. [2]

Cost

When it comes to creating your newspaper ad, there's the cost of designing the ad and placing it. You could have a simple *classified ad*, costing between $0.10 to $0.40 per word. Or you could create a *display ad*, which is based on column inches. These types of ads range from one to three inches at $8 to $20 per column inch.[3] For instance, if an ad were three inches by three inches, it'd equal nine column inches. If a column inch were $10, it'd be a $90 ad. While most newspapers have art departments to assist you with the ad, consider hiring a freelance designer who really knows how to make an ad that pops. Hiring a designer could run you from $150 to $500.

ASK!
Don't be afraid to negotiate. Most of the time, newspapers provide volume discounts if you commit to running a certain number of ads. You may also be able to negotiate first-time rate discounts.

The Free Papers
Think about advertising in **niche papers** as well—college newspapers and local business papers, for example. Sometimes, these free papers reach a larger audience because—yes, the obvious—THEY'RE FREE.

TIP 72

Ads in Hometown Magazines

Many towns or counties have local publications such as a town magazine. This can be a great place to advertise since a magazine is almost always kept around longer than a newspaper. Many local publications give free copies to local businesses such as banks, doctors' offices, and coffee shops where people may flip through these magazines while they're waiting or drinking their morning joe. An attractive ad can grab the attention of someone who wasn't even looking for a new salon. The size of the circulation will make a deciding factor whether to advertise weekly or monthly. It's also important to advertise three times in a row for market awareness. Best placement is in the first third of the magazine, on a right-hand page.

Cost

If you want to know the exact cost to advertise in a specific magazine, you need to contact the advertising department of that magazine and request a *Media Kit* and/or a *Rate Card*. If you commit to running an ad in more than one issue, you generally save on each individual ad. Say an ad was $1,000. If you run that ad in six issues, you may be able to negotiate to $750 per ad. There may also be setup costs associated in running an ad and for special placement.

Again, Don't Be Afraid to Ask!
You can negotiate with ad reps to get some extra perks. If you commit to a six-month run of an ad, for example, you may be able to get a few more months free. You may also be able to run your ad on the magazine's website for no extra charge or negotiate for special positioning (inside the covers or on the first few pages).

Time

Most of the time, magazines will desire a specific look for an ad, one that fits the publication's tone and target market. They will have a design department assist with your layout. Set aside a few hours to meet with them and to send a few emails back and forth to finalize the look of the ad.

Study Your Competitors
Study competitors' ads for inspiration (what TO do) and what NOT to do. Look at the language of the ads, the design, and the colors. Try to determine what's working and also how your salon/spa/barbershop is different. What makes your business unique? Catchy headlines, calls to action, these are all good things. Make sure your ads contain your contact information. Make it easy on the reader.

 The best way to find out about your competition is to go have services done there. Go get a service, ask questions, look around, but stay anonymous.

TIP 73

Coupon Mailings

Coupon and postcard mailings are another alternative to reach out to an exclusive target market and a good way to target a specific region within proximity of your salon's business. There are local coupon companies that mail out multiple businesses in their packet and companies like Vistaprint that guide you through the process of designing and mailing out postcards, including the purchasing of a targeted mailing list. These mailings are a very inexpensive way to target a market and a way to get introduced to other businesses that are advertising as well.

Valpak is a direct-mail company that's been around since the 60s. Most of us are familiar with its blue envelope full of glossy coupons. The company's main audience is "educated women ages 25–54 with incomes typically one-third higher than average." [1]

A benefit of postcard mailings is that people don't have to open up a letter; the information is right there for them to see when they pick up their mail. If the design is beautiful or the deal is amazing, they may even put it up on their fridge.

Cost

Valpak requires a run of 10,000 homes, with costs ranging from $150 to $400 per run. [2] For finer details, call Valpak directly. With postcard mailings, you need to take into account the costs of designing the postcard, printing the postcard, purchasing mailing lists, and postage. Vistaprint, for example, offers targeted mailing lists starting at $0.07 per name.

> **Target New Residents Before the Other Salons Have a Chance!**
> Sending out "Welcome to the Neighborhood" postcards with a free service for new residents is a great way to win customers. You can purchase mailing lists targeted to new residents through places like Vistaprint's "Movers & New Homeowners" lists, which start at $0.18 per name. [3]

Time

Companies like Valpak have designers on staff to assist with your ad. You will need to provide your logo and some pictures. Having ideas before you get on the phone will save you time and money. This should take no more than four to five hours.

TIP 74

The Yellow Pages

"Calls to businesses from Yellow Pages ads have a 50 percent conversion rate, compared with 3 percent for online."
—Dennis R. Fromholzer, PhD, President, CRM Associates [1]

Don't believe the hype. The Yellow Pages are used as more than just a doorstopper. A lot of people still respect and trust this old-fashioned directory, especially for services like finding a hairstylist or an electrician. The consumers who turn to the Yellow Pages first are older consumers who have always used them, but even younger consumers who would normally search their smartphone still grab the printed directory as a backup if they have a slow Internet connection or if the phonebook is close by. And the older generation, 65 and over, is a large segment most salons shouldn't neglect. Even one of Google's top dogs, Matt Cutts, is on record saying we shouldn't neglect this classic. [2]

Cost

Expect to pay a couple hundred dollars for a listing, depending on whether you're just listing your name and contact information or taking out a larger box ad in black and white or color. But you can pay once and be done with it. You can also negotiate with the salesperson. See if you can be listed in a second category or get a free online advertisement as well.

Time

This should take no more than two hours to settle on what you want to say, how your ad will look, and where you want it to be placed.

TIP 75

Distribution of Marketing Materials

Flyers and brochures can still make an impact in bringing your salon/spa/barbershop to the attention of the masses.

Pass out brochures to local partner businesses, schools, real estate agents, apartment complexes, bridal stores, etc. Post flyers in coffee shops, grocery stores, and college campuses. Make sure the flyers have takeaway coupons on them with your business's contact information.

Bathrooms: Make Sure Your Name Is Not on the Wall...

Get creative with your posting places. An especially good idea is posting in places where people are forced to sit or stand with nothing else to do but read your flyer, like bathrooms and bus stations.

Cost

This should be one of the cheapest ways to let people know you're in business. Printing 100–500 flyers at standard color at a place like Staples shouldn't run more than $100–$200. Fancy flyers will run you more. Prices at the time of this book start at $0.42 (1–50 flyers) for standard color and $0.085 (1–100 flyers) for black and white. Per-piece prices go down the more flyers ordered.

Time

Have one of your kids or a college student design a flyer for your salon business. You can find them by placing an ad on Craigslist or putting an ad in their student newspaper. This should take no more than two hours. Or, if one of your stylists is artistically inclined, have him or her design the flyer for an incentive.

TIP 76

Signage

"Advertising is, of course, important because advertise is the final design. It's the last layer that speaks to the customer, that tells them what you have and what you offer."
—Tom Ford

There is no better way to let people know what you do or what your business offers than to have a great sign. While we focus much of our advertising dollars on reaching our target customers, we forget about the people right in front of our noses—passersby and drivers.

Attract the Men

Barber's pole equals *We Cut Men's Hair.* If you're a salon or spa that does men's hair, add one. Make it easy on the guys; attract them with the pole. An illuminated sign in your window will let would-be customers know that they are welcome to come in and browse or check out any daily promotions you may be running on services or retail products. This sign can be updated as often as you like.

> **IMPORTANT:** Make sure your town and landlord allow for your sign. Sometimes there are restrictions.

Cost

An illuminated LED window sign can range from $50 to $300 based on the size. What's nice about these signs is that you can change the message daily. A barber's pole ranges in price from $500 to $1,500.

Time

You can find either of these items online. This should take you no more than an hour to pick and choose the sign or barber's pole for your business. Amazon and eBay are good places to start.

Questions to Consider When Choosing Your Sign and Where to Place It

- Will your town and landlord allow you to put a barber's pole outside your business? If not, you may have to get creative. Use your window space to permanently display a barber's pole from the inside of your barbershop. Or, incorporate a barber's pole in the artwork for your barbershop sign.
- Will your sign be visible from all directions?
- Will your sign attract new clients?
- Will your sign "brand" your barbershop (or salon/spa/etc.)?
- Is your sign appealing and legible?
- Can you put your logo on the sign?
- Does it need to be illuminated?
- Will it block your windows?
- Is there any obstruction or part of the building that limits its size?

SWEETENING THE DEAL

TIP 77

Promotions and Special Events

"People will buy anything that is 'one to a customer.'"
—Sinclair Lewis

Just as sales draw people to a store, promotions and events draw people to salons, spas, and barbershops. Draw people to your salon because it has happening events and sweet deals, hot talent and fresh looks; make your salon the "it" salon.

Promotions

In today's world, everyone is looking to save money and still feel special. How many times have we done a double take when we've seen a special sale or picked up two of an item we weren't even planning on buying because it's currently BOGO (buy one, get one free)? Promotions are attention-getters. They're often one-time specials you offer in order to promote your business. They may be things you give away in order to attract new customers or to generate goodwill and loyalty among your existing customers—even to woo back absent clients. Promotions are similar to advertising in that there is a cost involved. In the case of promotions, the cost is most likely to be a free or discounted service. If you have slow days or stylists with unbooked time, this may be a more manageable cost than spending green dollars on advertising. And once you get these potential customers into your salon, they won't be able to resist coming back for more.

Keep this core value in mind: promotions are a way to make clients feel special. Offer first customers a free consultation or a discounted haircut or color, even a welcome package. Reward returning clients a monetary incentive off their third or fourth visit. On every visit, ask your clients if they would like to try a new product; if they say yes, discount it 10 percent. If clients use the product and don't like it, allow them to return it for an exchange, or it's not only *what* promotions you offer but also *how* you offer them that makes them special to the client. Paying attention and getting to know your target and current clients allows you to tailor promotions to their personal tastes.

Special Events

Make your salon/spa/barbershop the "it" place to be by hosting fun, unique events.

Hosting beauty, grooming, and makeover events can be a great way to bring in customers who were not aware that you existed, and you can tailor these events to the season, current trends, blockbuster movies—the possibilities are endless. Special events are usually made available to anyone and are posted on marketing materials and the salon's website and social media. Events are also a great way to promote new products and service offerings—usually at a discount. These types of events give guests the ability to try something new without spending as much—and everyone wants to save money but still have fun!

Promote New Stylists and Barbers!
Events are also a fun way to promote new stylists and barbers and build their book of business while increasing employee morale.

Look into an in-store raffle or giveaway, and advertise the event as widely as your budget will allow. Make your promotional event exciting and different, get your retail product people involved, and invite the mayor or other important people in town. Make your salon's event the event not to miss. Make sure you have plenty of staff on hand to meet and greet everyone.

Involve Your Partners
Events are also a great partner activity—plan and throw an event together, and immediately you're having an entirely new influx of potential customers—your partner's. Share your customers! Mix it up!

Save Money—Use Your Vendors/Product Salespeople!
These folks will save you tons. You can have your product salesperson bring in sales promotions, samples, or special-deal signage for the salon.

Promotions and Events
Time and Money
Potential Investments

Time

- Time to brainstorm events and promotions
- Time to plan the event
- Time to reach out to partners for shared events
- Time to speak with vendors and ask for freebies and signage
- Time to create marketing materials for the event or promotion
- Time to distribute said materials or to reach out to traditional marketing avenues
- Time to update social media to build buzz for the event or promotion
- Time to follow up with new customers; repeat business is the goal
- Time to post pics and brag on the event

Money

- Cost of discounted or free services or products
- Printing costs (for frequent customer cards, referral cards, etc.)
- Cards for special events and postage
- Cost of mailing lists and postage to reach out to new residents
- Raffle items
- Cost of any traditional advertising methods used to promote the event
- Sandwichboard (to advertise outside your building)

- Cost of a street team to build buzz and hand out materials (could be your own staff, friends, or college kids willing to work for pizza or a discounted service, or you could hire a professional team
- Cost for welcome baskets for new customers
- Referral fees if you use a service like Groupon
- Food and drink
- Decorations
- Additional entertainment (band, magician, etc.)
- Smartphone or good digital camera to take pics
- Stamps and cards to send a personal thank you to new customers
- Costume rentals for seasonal events

TIP 78

Hire a Street Team

Consider hiring or building a street team to promote your salon and its specials. Radio stations use them, bands use them, so why not use them to promote your salon to the community? You can build up your own team from enthusiastic, friendly people you know (friends or family) or college students (put an ad in the college newspaper or on Craigslist), treating them to pizza or a free service for their time. Or, you can hire street-promotion professionals from sites such as http://nationalstreetteams.com/ or http://www.eventprostrategies.com. Arm your street team with promotional materials, and direct them to high-traffic locations where your target customers gather. This can be a great way to build real buzz for your salon, especially if business really needs a boost. Also, be sure to include a way to gather contact information from potential customers.

> **Social Media Buzz! Go Viral!**
> If your street team includes a clever, creative element in their promotional activities, people may take pics with their smartphones and upload to Instagram, Facebook, whatever. Your salon could go viral, meaning the pics would be viewed and shared by a massive amount of people in a short period of time.

Street marketing can take some planning. Where are your target customers gathering? What time of the day are they there? What are the solicitation rules? Are permits needed for your local municipality? Then, you need to build the team and pick a date that's good for all. There's also the printing of promotional items and any other creative planning involved.

> **IMPORTANT:** Some places prohibit solicitation (selling), so keep this in mind when picking places for your street marketing team. It's important to know the town's rules for solicitation; the last thing your salon needs is trouble from local authorities.

TIP 79

Fun Daily and Weekly Specials

Start running daily or weekly deals on products or services that can afford to discount (we're in the business of making money, so make sure the discount makes financial sense). Think quick blowouts or updos, or retail that isn't moving or that you can get at a super discount from your product supplier.

Come up with some good ideas at your weekly staff meeting. Make it fun, and spread the word through your existing customer base. The word will get out around town through your clients and staff and will surely influence new customers to try out the salon.

Ideas for Weekly Specials

You could have a week full of specials, such as the following:

Monday: *Manic Mondays:* manicures for $20; *Makeover Mondays:* 15 percent off products

Tuesday: *Color Tuesdays:* $10 off any color service

Wednesday: *Winebar Wednesdays:* complimentary glass of wine and $5 off any service

Thursday: *Throwback Thursdays:* bring in an old pic of yourself (the crazier the hair and makeup, the better) and get 15 percent off your service; *Thirsty Thursdays:* complimentary beer with $10 off a service

Friday: *Friendly Fridays:* bring in a friend and you each receive 20 percent off your service; *Date-Night Fridays:* blowouts for $25

Change It Up!
Change it up every now and again, like wearing a new dress and new lipstick or new shirt and kicks, and promote like crazy. Put flyers up. Post on social media. Having fun daily or weekly deals will keep your clients visiting your pages to see what's new and if their favorite service is on special that week.

TIP 80

Blackboard Special

"In good times, people want to advertise; in bad times, they have to."
—Bruce Barton

We've all seen a blackboard in front of a restaurant offering today's lunch or dinner specials, so why can't a salon do the same thing? Buy a nice, strong easel and blackboard that can withstand the wind and display outside of your salon. Offer a blackboard special, including the sentence "Walk-Ins Welcome." This is a very inexpensive way to say, "Come on in and give us a try; we would love to have you."

Use brightly colored chalk, and write legibly. If you have a stylist who rocks at artwork, put them in charge of the blackboard.

Go Viral!
Creative blackboard messages and designs make their way onto people's phones and social media. Have fun with this!

You can find a decent blackboard with stand for about $100. You'll also need some colored chalk.

TIP 81

Sale Days—LIMITED TIME ONLY!

Why is it that once you're *un*available, the guys and gals start beating down the door? People want what's harder to have. The thrill of the chase . . . whatever you call it.

The same goes with sales.

There's an urgency there—if you don't grab it now, you're missing out. Think of how department stores do it. They use words that inspire urgency and a call to action. Think *limited-time only*, *three-day sale*, *grand opening!* Pick up a Sunday paper and look at the store ads. Make the invite seem as if they miss it, the promotion will never come back again.

The great thing is that technology has made it so much easier to alert your customers to these sales. You should have a database full of customer emails, so do an email blast with a coupon. Or do a text-message blast to those who sign up for the service. Send a newsletter once a month. Invite your customers to share the message/deal with their friends and family.

TIP 82

Seasonal Events

Think of the seasons and the necessary needs, protections, and preparations needed for each. Then, offer specials on related products and services, and plan some fun events.

End-of-Season Events and Promotions
Have **end-of-season** events and promotions as well. Great way to move products off the shelf for new inventory.

Seasonal Ideas

Here are some seasonal beauty topics of interest and "issues" you may be able to solve. Think of what products and services you can provide to help your customers look and feel their best year-round.

Spring/Summer
Protecting hair from chlorine, saltwater, and harsh chemicals
Sunburned skin
Sweatproof makeup
Getting rid of unwanted hair (it is bathing suit season)
Fresh, easy haircuts and styles
Sandal-ready feet

Summer's Over
Replenishing dry, damaged hair
Maintaining the summer glow

Back to School
Trying a new look

Classy makeup
Easy haircuts for busy mornings
Massages for stress relief

Fall/Winter
Protecting our skin from the elements
Dry, flaky skin
Moisturizing our hair to avoid flyaways
Holiday stress

The list goes on and on. Solving client beauty issues and helping them look and feel great year-round is your duty.

Off-Season Specials
Some services, such as tanning, are more popular at certain times of the year. To maintain interest in the off-season, offer some "can't-miss-out" specials. If you offer tanning, for instance, have a "Look Tan Before the Summer" promo. Give buy one, get one tans.

TIP 83

Add Pumpkin to Your Menu: The Power of The Season

Everyone knows the seasons are fun. We get to make a snowman, go trick or treating, smell the flowers, go to the beach, we look forward to the seasons. Add a little season to your salon. Change your menu and make it specific to the season.

TIP 84

Holiday Promotions and Events

Christmas, Valentine's Day, Easter, July 4th, and other holidays are ideal times to invite people to your salon/spa/barbershop. And printed personal invitations are excellent ways to make your customers feel special, especially during the holidays. Make it a holiday celebration in the salon. Ask each guest to bring a friend. Give out holiday treats and gift bags. If you're packed around Christmas, pick a less-busy holiday when you'd like to increase traffic and people are more likely to be free.

Holiday Ideas

Brainstorm all the different holidays and fun specials and events that could go along with them.

Some ideas:

- May Is for Moms (Mother's Day)
- June Is for Dads (Father's Day)
- Valentine's Day
- Veterans Day
- Administrative Professionals Week
- Earth Day
- Tax Day (okay, not a holiday—not fun AT ALL—but think stress-relief specials)
- Hanukkah

The list goes on an on. You'll notice there is a holiday for EVERYTHING. Heck, your salon/spa/barbershop could even come up with a holiday of its own!

Post these holiday promotions and events on social media. Make your specials unique and plan them regularly, and people will be visiting your social media and salon more often.

TIP 85

Christmas

Christmas is a biggie for sales; retailers depend on the sales from Black Friday up to Christmas to reach quotas and budgets. You too should be taking advantage of this spend-happy season. People are looking for great gifts for their friends, family, coworkers, clients, the mailman—and also wanting to look stunning or suave for all their swanky holiday events. Be their go-to place for hot deals and the hottest looks.

Promote every day on your social media, and post fun pics of your staff and clients in the holiday spirit and rocking stunning holiday styles. Also meet with your product salesperson who may be able to offer you free signage and samples for holiday goodie bags.

Have fun with the season. You could have a "Styling Santa" contest in which your stylists compete to style Santa—dyeing his hair red or green, teasing it, wherever inspiration takes them. Let people vote for the most styling Santa. This would be a fun event to advertise and would draw lots of attention. Have goodies on hand and some swag to give those who attend.

Make It Easy on Customers

The Christmas season can be stressful, so make your salon/spa/barbershop as Zen as possible for your clients.

- Offer e-gift cards and the means to purchase services and products online.
- Provide free shipping and overnight delivery.
- Provide free gift-wrapping in the store.
- Offer holiday-themed gift cards.
- Have great sales customers won't be able to resist.

- Consider two-for-ones or free services, free products, or free sample deals if customers purchase a gift for their loved ones.
- Have gift ideas, including stocking stuffers, on display to make it easy on customers. Retail hair products, makeup, and brushes make for great gift ideas.
- Make your salon itself a happy place to be with goodies, friendly staff, and yummy scents.

TIP 86

Themed Promotions and Events

Everybody want to be in the movies, experience the glamor and glitz. What about the Roaring Twenties? A book and movie like *The Great Gatsby* conspires to make the 99 percent forget about credit-card debt, problems at work, and family issues. It makes you feel like you want to join the rich in a shopping spree, a night on the town, or a day at the beauty salon. Maybe for just one hour or two you can make your customers feel like they entered the life of the rich and famous. Glamor! Excess! Hedonism! Set the stage by turning your salon into the set of the Gatsby era. Dress in gowns, have all your staff turn into the characters, and have fun with it! It will be a day and night for your customers to remember. Promote the event and post pictures on all your social media channels. Encourage the sale of products that help customers achieve the hair and makeup looks of the decade. Go a step further and post step-by-step pics and videos.

So much fun could be had with decades—pin curls, high ponytails, pomade, big eighties hair—the list is endless.

In business, this is called *nostalgia marketing*. Think of Pepsi and its Throwback series, Wendy's "Where's the Beef?" campaign, and McDonalds and the sale of Coca-Cola glasses or its bringing back the McRib sandwich.

Decade, or nostalgia, events are a win-win for all ages. They bring back happy memories for the older crowd and are retro-cool to the younger.

TIP 87

Movies, TV, and Books Tie-In Promotions and Events

If there's a movie, TV show, or book that is getting a lot of attention—or even a classic that's still going strong—why not host an event or a promotion to tie in with it, one that focuses on bringing its styles and looks to life? These events could be for all ages.

Braids became popular after the Disney movie *Frozen*, so you could do a promotion on braids or a *Frozen*-themed event with braiding lessons. For guys, what about a *Goodfellas* or *Godfather* event to showcase your products? Show the gents how to use your pomades to get those retro-cool looks the ladies will love. Maybe do a *Steel Magnolias* event for the ladies (or pick ANY 80s movie), and have fun with big hair. Or what about shows like *Mad Men* that brought 60s style to the forefront? So many possibilities. Have fun with it.

If you host an event, take lots of pictures and post on social media. Ham it up with clothes and foods that match the time period. If promoting a product or service, ham it up too. If offering a special on braids a la *Frozen*, post clips from the movie next to customers all done up with their pretty braids. Barbers, post pics of your "goodfellas" looking cool a la amazing product that is 20 percent off this month.

Keep your eyes and ears open to the current trends in culture, and also consider classic and cult movies (*Pretty in Pink? The Breakfast Club? Pulp Fiction?*). Make your salon/spa/barbershop the most fun place to be—a place that allows its clients to live the dream of their favorite movies, shows, and books!

Friendly Competition!
Make this idea more fun by having your clients and those on social media vote for their favorite movie hair—the movie with the most votes wins the themed event. Or you could have costume contests or a vote-for-your-favorite whatever. People love a little friendly competition.

TIP 88

Fun, Creative Package Deals

Think of creative ways to package your services. Packages could win you more business and profits because they just SOUND FUN—read: HARD TO RESIST!

Some ideas:
- **Date-night packages** (blowouts, style, makeup, manicure, etc.)
- **Stress-relief packages** (massage, facial, etc.)
- **Fountain-of-youth packages** (hair coloring, facials, exfoliation, oil treatments, etc.)
- **Summer-ready packages** (deep conditioning, waxing, mani/pedis, etc.)
- **Winter-ready packages** (moisturizing treatments for skin and hair, etc.)

You could include products or product discounts in these packages as well.

TIP 89

Roll Out a New Line of Products or Colors

If your distributor is offering education to your staff, invite some of your clients. Let them try a new service, or use them as models. And when the new products hit the shelf, promote them like crazy. Post pics on social media of stylists and clients using the product or their styles after using the product—this goes for both men and women. You could even create an event to celebrate the unveiling of a new product line or series of colors. Think of brands/companies like OPI and its constant unveiling of new colors under a theme. Have fun with your product promotions. You could tie them in under a theme of your own.

TIP 90

Monthly Specials

Just like the employee of the month, what about these ideas?
- Product of the month
- Style of the month
- Color of the month
- __ of the month (Come up with your own idea!)

Promote the monthly deal everywhere. This is a great way to bring attention to a new product or service or one that isn't selling.

Promote New Employees!
If you have a new barber or stylist, make him or her the focus of the month. Spread the word with some extra promotions and discounts for the month. Think Groupon, think Facebook, think all the ways you can promote them on social media.

TIP 91

Quickie Services

With people always on the move, it's important to offer quick, on-the-go services. An extra bonus to customers: these services are cheaper. Come up with a clever name for these services, and let your customers know it'll only take 10 minutes to come into the salon and give one of the treatments a try. But if they don't know about these services, they won't come. Spread the word and offer a free mini service for first-time customers including current customers who have never tried the service.

Quickie Ideas

- Blowout
- Deep-conditioning treatment
- Facial
- Massages
- Bang trim
- Beard trim
- Makeup fixer
- False-eyelash application
- Eyebrow waxing

What are some services you could create smaller and more-affordable versions of? Create a separate section of your menu for these services, and promote them like crazy. You'll soon be seeing an increase in visits from your current clients and new ones.

TIP 92

Frequent-Service Punch Cards

Airlines do it. Restaurants do it. Coffee shops do it. No reason salons and barbershops can't do it, too. Do what? *Reward your customers for repeat visits.* Print some "Frequent Color" cards with your logo and spaces to punch out or initial each visit. Or choose the service you make the most money on or are trying to promote. After the 10th visit, the customer gets a free or discounted service. The nice thing about doing it this way instead of just automatically giving customers something on their 10th visit is that the customer thinks about being rewarded every time he or she pulls out the card. The card also stays in his wallet or her purse and may get shown to friends.

> To expand your market base, give the client a different service for free after the 10th visit, such as after 10 haircuts, get one free facial—or you could do five services, get one free. It's up to you; it's your business. But this way, customers are trying something new as well, something they'll probably love and—bingo!—more appointments.

TIP 93

Customer-Referral Cards and Rewards

If you do a great job on someone's hair, everyone's going to be asking: Who did your hair? That makes your happy customer even happier, and it turns them into a walking, talking advertisement for you, so why not use that to your advantage and let your loyal customer earn a perk at the same time.

Give your happy customers referral cards. Have the customer put his or her name on it to receive credit for the referral (and larger rewards for multiple referrals). The new customer gets 10–20 percent off a first-time service (haircut, color, etc.) with you. Design the reward program to fit your salon's budget. You can print out these cards in-house or through an online or local print service (like Vistaprint or Staples). Be sure to reward your customers who bring in multiple referrals , but don't just offer them a free service, give them a gift card good for anything in the salon.

Let Technology Do the Work
Today's POS systems offer loyalty-tracking programs on them. The receptionist can have fun with it: "Sir, it's your ninth visit, you're almost there." (**Product Plug:** Consider Meevo by Millennium S.I. beauty management software: www.meevo.com.)

TIP 94

Friends-and-Family Certificates

These are similar to referral cards, but instead of the customer giving out cards, you send something directly to the customer's friends and family. Ask your happy customers if they have friends and family who'd like a $10 gift certificate to see you. Gather their information, and then send these friends and family a nice, personalized letter or card with the gift certificate, compliments of their friend/family member and your salon. Send your customer a thank you and gift certificate as well. Personal referrals go a long way; we trust the opinions of our friends and family more than a stranger's or a sales ad.

This is a surefire way to get new customers at very little expense.

TIP 95

Birthday Program

Rewarding customers on their birthday is a great way to build loyalty and even grow your customer base. Give existing customers a discounted service, or better yet a free or deeply discounted product (small, sample, or travel sized products are perfect for that). You can even offer them a pampering party to ensure they bring in a friend or two for a day of services and glam.

Today's awesome software programs have the capability to keep track of customer birthdays, sending out emails and texts to remind them to come in for their free or discounted service. If you want an extra-special touch, send your customers—especially VIP customers—a paper birthday card through the mail.

TIP 96

Celebrate Salon Anniversaries

Anniversaries aren't just for dating and married couples! Celebrate salon anniversaries—the 6-month mark, 1-year date, 2-year date, etc. after your customer's initial visit. Just as you collect your customer's birthday, also record your customer's first visit.

Then, start a program to celebrate these special days with your customer. You could send a card saying something like, "Happy anniversary! It's been a year (two years, etc.) since your first visit to our salon. As a thank you for your business, come in for a free haircut!"

Celebrating your customers is a great way to retain them and guarantee they will share these experiences with their friends and family, meaning new customers may come out of this too. Each stylist/barber/massage therapist, etc. should take ownership of this with his or her book of clients.

TIP 97

Celebrate VIP Clients

Shameless Plug
Check out our book *How to Offer 5-Star Service at Your Salon*. This book will help you take your customer service to the 5-star level, adding that "wow" factor that draws in clients and keeps them coming back.

There's a small percentage of clients you will consider VIPs. These clients should be treated as such, and a special program should be implemented just for them. VIP clients can be loyal clients who've been coming to you for years or those who spend tons of money on services on a regular basis (the ones who keep your lights on). Keep these folks happy, and show them how much you appreciate them. Whether it's a discount or a gift card, these customers must be paid attention to. These VIP offerings will be a great form of advertising for new clients, too. Remember, your best customers spread the word.

Treat these clients like the stars they are. Take a gorgeous picture of them, and post it on your website and Facebook page along with the tag "VIP Customer" and a few kind words.

TIP 98

Celebrate New Moms and Dads

New moms and dads are TIRED, so pamper them a little. Send them a "Congratulations on the New Baby" card with a gift certificate for a free or heavily discounted service. Be a family-friendly place of business.

Celebrate! Celebrate!
Make your salon the fun place to be because you're always celebrating its most important people—your customers. The more you give, the more you receive. (Just stay within budget.)

TIP 99

Senior Discount

Seniors love the social aspect of their salon or barbershop, coming frequently not only to be pampered but also (and probably more) for the social aspect of being out of the house and part of something special. And, let's face the facts, no matter how old we get, we still want to look good. There is nothing better than a haircut, makeup, or a facial to make anyone feel special and youthful again.

So make the senior crowd feel good, but keep in mind that they may be on a fixed income and budget. They want a place to go, but only if the price is right.

You can advertise in your local newspaper or Valpak or simply put a sign out in front of your salon. We talked about blackboard specials earlier, this would be a great place to let seniors know. How about the bulletin board at the local grocery store with a tear-off? Or make a personal visit to the local senior centers and drop off some salon menus and coupons. Letting seniors know they are welcome is an open invitation for not only one but many, as seniors usually travel in packs.

TIP 100

Catch New Residents First

Catch new residents while they're still unpacking. No, don't show up at their door and bother them, but think about it, when people move to town, they have a checklist of things they need to do, and finding a new stylist is on this list. Think how tired they must be from moving and how they deserve a little pampering. Spoil these newbies; make them just HAVE to come in for a free or deeply discounted service.

So how to find the newbies in your town? Well, you can purchase mailing lists targeted to new residents through places like Vistaprint's Movers & New Homeowners lists, which start at $0.18 per name.[1] You can also enlist the help of a company such as www.welcomematservices.com that focuses on helping businesses reach new residents.

You may have to shell out a little dough to find these new residents, but it's worth it. Ponder the fact that you're reaching fresh folks who are actively looking for stylists (they're unattached and available), and most people stick with one stylist/barber once they've found one they like. Shop around to find the best companies and prices to help you make these mailing lists or to do the work for you.

Ask around if there are newcomers' groups sponsored by a civic group (like the Chamber of Commerce' local Visitors/Tourism Bureau, newspaper or a religious group). Often these newcomers groups have speakers, mixers, and get-togethers where you may be welcome to come, introduce yourself, and plug your business. Even if they don't, the host or sponsor will typically provide newcomers with a welcome packet, so see how your salon, spa, or barbershop can be listed in there.

Targeted Mailings
While the post office direct-mail program only tailors to zip codes and not new residents, consider using a targeted mailing if there's a large, new development in the area.

TIP 101

Celebrate New Customers with a Welcome Package or Gift

Create a welcome kit for each new client who comes to your salon. This does not have to be expensive, but make it special. It might include some product samples, chocolate, tea or coffee, and a coupon for a return visit. People tend to stay with a trusted stylist or barber for years, so taking the time to woo your new customers is important.

The cost depends on what you decide to put in the package. See if you can get your product supplier to pitch in and give you free samples, brushes, etc. The cost of a bag with your salon logo plus the items you put in it should not exceed $30.

TIP 102

Giveaways and Freebies

Giveaways and freebies are a great way to win the attention of new clients and build loyalty with your current clients.

Larger prizes especially draw a lot of attention. A big TV or trip giveaway will have gossip spreading quickly amongst your customers. For example, sell $1 raffle tickets for a big prize (like that TV); draw the raffle the day before Christmas or a big holiday, and you should be able to pay for the unit from the raffles and create a lot of new business.

You could also collaborate on a raffle for big-ticket items or gift baskets with your partners. Draw the ticket at a fun event, and get the media involved. Can the radio station attend the event? Radio advertising can draw lots of attention. Also, promote like mad on social media channels.

Social Media Giveaways
Gain the attention of even more potential clients by running a Facebook or Twitter raffle. In this case, you're not asking for money, only that participants share and like the post (Facebook) or retweet the post (Twitter) to enter the drawing. This is a great way to get your name out there.

TIP 103

Tips for Slow Nights or Days

If you've got a night or day when business is pretty slow, why not roll out one of your salon's specialties for a bargain price or give out some free services? Make it a regular thing, and you'll soon see business booming. Offer eyebrow waxing for $5 or free blowouts.

Promote these specials and theme nights heavily via social media. And think of teaming up with sites like Groupon and LivingSocial, which send their subscribers hot daily deals via email.

TIP 104

Makeover Mondays

Monday is normally the slowest day for a salon; in fact, most are closed. So why not use Mondays as your "Makeover Monday"?

Offer discounted services and free makeovers to your existing clients, and ask them to bring in a guest for a makeover. Use these Monday makeovers for your slowest stylists. This will surely assist in building their books of business. Get your distributor involved so that he or she can assist with free samples or education for your clients.

If you make Mondays enticing to your current and new customers, you may just find that the lack of salon competition coupled with your fun events and mad skills make this day your busiest day of the week.

TIP 105

Open on Sundays

Not only is Monday a slow day but Sunday usually is too. Most salons are closed on these days. So being open makes you immediately ahead of the competition.

For Sundays, focus on women. On this day most men are watching football (yeah, there are ladies who love sports but lots more who don't—just being real here). So a "Girls Day" could be a perfect way to attract the ladies. How about a pedicure party for two to four friends at $15 per person or facials discounted 30 percent off regular price? Create a "pampering party," and offer a free glass of wine with some snacks. Sunday can be a very profitable day; you just need to focus on attracting the right client.

TIP 106

Neighborhood Meet and Greet

Years ago, people sat on their porches on summer nights and talked with the neighbors. Now, we're more likely to stay inside, binge-watch sitcoms, and text message those across the room. So why not break the mold and host a neighborhood meet and greet? What a great way for all of the merchants in your area to get to know each other and understand what each of you do. You might even decide to partner with some of them, helping each other grow your book of business.

Make it a must that each merchant local business brings 10 of its best clients to meet with everyone in your shopping area. Keep in mind this works best in a shopping mall, strip mall, or main street in town. And other businesses must be willing to work on the event with you to promote it. This will take some time to plan and orchestrate, but if you get all the businesses to pick a day, night, or weekend to have this special meet-your-neighbor event, it could be a big win for everyone. Make it special, have some wine and cheese, and offer those 10-minute quickies we spoke about earlier.

Businesses in Residential Areas
If your business is located in a residential area, talk with the homeowner association or apartment-complex manager about partnering with them on a meet-and-greet.

TIP 107

Girls'-Night-Out Promotions and Events

Since this is about girls going out, choose an evening near the weekend—Thursday makes sense—and have specials on going-out/date-night services. What about blowouts for 25 percent off that evening? This gives your client beautiful hair for the weekend and increases Thursday traffic in your salon. You could also do a Friday or Saturday event and have cheap makeovers or eyelash extensions, mani/pedi deals, etc.

If you want to do a girls'-night-out event, there are so many possibilities. You could have giveaways donated from your partners, serve wine from a local winery, have appetizers or desserts on hand, play some fun music, and give each attendee a bag with the salon name and product samples—just make it fun.

Get Your Partners Involved, and Bring In Some New Clients!
If you are partnered with a massage therapist or fitness studio, for example, you could have them join in and give mini massages or an exercise or yoga lesson. Have them invite their customers to the event. There are tons of ways to involve your partners, which brings in their clients (potential new customers for you.) while also promoting their business to yours.

TIP 108

Handbag Swap

Most women love their handbags. Yet, over time, even the most prized handbag loses its allure with the person who purchased it. So have a handbag swap in your salon or spa. Make some signs for your front desk, announce the event on your social media, and let your staff talk it up with clients. You will need to pump up this event for at least a month to let everyone know about it. What a fun way to swap out what once was your beloved designer handbag for a new bag that someone else once cherished. You can also get the local boutiques involved. If they carry a handbag line, they'd probably be more than happy to split expenses, promote the event, and share their client lists. Have some wine, cheese, and snacks on hand to make the event special. Also give away some coupons to prospective clients.

Clothing Swap
You could also do a clothing swap and donate whatever is left to the local women's shelter.

TIP 109

Beard Events

So much fun can be had with beards. They are big, and they are back.

Think . . .
- Beards and barbecue
- Beards and beer
- Bluegrass, bourbon, and beards
- Beard-growing contest
- Weird-beard event
- Bearded-lady event (oh, that could get interesting.)
- Beards of Denver (or whatever your city is)
- Beards and bands
- Bad-ass beards

Make the event fun. Promote it heavily—draw attention to this fun, unique event. Add some pizza or barbecue and fun games like Cornhole if you have the space outside. But remember to keep the focus on beards: proper grooming, great products, trimmers and styling tools, and, of course, tips to keep a beard healthy and luxurious.

TIP 110

Father/Son and Mother/Daughter Events

These events can be as simple as offering 50 percent off the second person if they both come in. The week before or the month of Mother's Day and Father's Day is an especially good time to have these specials. You can also add special touches such as tea and cookies and a free flower for the moms. For dads, how about free pizza, soda, and beer and a complimentary product or promotional item with the salon's or barbershop's name on it?

TIP 111

Military Discount

Military discounts are a great way to pay back in a small way the young men and women who serve or have served in the military to protect our country. Post a sign in the salon and in the salon's window that every day is discount day for active and retired military. Once the word spreads around your area that military personnel are welcome and get a discount, you should immediately see results with new clients.

> **Businesses Near a Military Base**
> If your salon or barbershop is near a military base, offer military cuts for a good price, and promote them heavily. Let this become a specialty.

TIP 112

Night to Honor Those in Uniform

This is another easy one: honor the firemen, cops and paramedics in your uniform. Like with military personnel and veterans, offer these civil servants a discount. Pay them a visit where they work, bringing some snacks and treats and, of course, a stack of coupons good for a free first-time haircut. Spend some time with them, talking and getting friendly, don't just drop off the snacks and coupons and run.

TIP 113

Wine Tasting or Craft Beer Night

Have a wine or craft beer tasting through some local vendors. Call them up, tell them you are expecting 50 to 100 people, and ask if they will supply the wine or beer for free in exchange for selling their products at the tasting (or you could pay a fee for the service). This is good for both sides: the vendor gets to sell its wine or beer and gain new clients, and the salon benefits from the event, selling packages and services. You could even win some new customers loyal to the brewer. Have fun with this; you might make Wednesday or Thursday happy hours: Wine Wednesdays or Thirsty Thursdays. You're promoting a local winery or craft brewery, and it's promoting you.

If you can't get a distributor or bar to participate, don't sweat it, just head to your best local wine store or craft beer shop, pick up some bottles, and put on a tasting yourself.

Barbershops!
Craft beer nights or happy hours are a great idea for a barbershop.

TIP 114

Have a Fashion Show

You could try hosting your own fashion show. By working alongside your partners businesses and other local businesses, you can make this a great event.

You'll need to plan this event months in advance, and sell tickets through the local businesses that are displaying their products. Make sure you are fully staffed to meet and greet and book appointments with new and existing clients. Let your local newspaper and radio stations know about the event. Hang flyers around town, and promote on social media. All the models used in the fashion show should have amazing hair (styled by yours truly) and also wear the clothes from the partner boutiques involved. Another option is charging the vendors that display their product a fee for the event and letting your clients come in for free, instead of charging the customer a ticket. This will allow the client to spend more money with the vendors or on salon services.

Themed Fashion Shows

Themed shows always work. Here are some ideas:

- Bridal shows
- Prom
- Business-professional style (job interviews, etc.)
- Back-to-school trends
- Work-from-home styles
- Stylish maternity wear
- Make over my husband

- Makeover shows (in general)
- Fountain-of-youth shows (nursing homes and retirement communities would be great audiences)

Putting on a Fashion Show can be a big undertaking, so make sure you're prepared for a lot of work (and a lot of payoff) as you plan it. It may be worth the money (pulled together from all the partners) to hire an event coordinator or someone with experience in planning an event like this.

TIP 115

Image Makeovers

The world is constantly changing, and how we look, dress and feel is now more important than ever. With the power of the Internet, your clients have no boundaries when it comes to being on top of the newest fashion trends, stay-young potions, and looks of celebrities around the world. The demand for worldly knowledge of what's hot and what's not is now an extension of our values, our art, and the way we see the world and ourselves in it.

So why not offer your clients image makeovers? You can offer these to every client in the salon or to the clients you think may need it (or, should we say, those who look *to you* for style). Become known as the *Makeover Salon*. Specialize in the hottest trends, cuts, and fashion statements today. Have packages with different services that tailor to different kinds of makeovers.

Post Before-and-After Pictures
This is the best part of watching those makeover shows—the before-and-after pictures. Ask clients if you can take before-and-after pics and post on your site. Everyone loves makeover shows, and these kinds of dramatic before-and-after pics can really draw people in the doors. If they did it for her and him, what can Ms. Stylist and Mr. Barber do *for me*?

You could also host a makeover hair/makeup/grooming/fashion show of your own; in this case, consider your partner businesses.

TIP 116

Beauty/Grooming How-To's and Wellness Seminars

Why not have a special event catering to the latest styles and trends, showing customers how to make a perfect fishtail braid or how to wear the newest makeup shades of the season? Barbershops can offer grooming workshops or how-to's for the hottest new styles in mens' grooming. Promote a new stylist by having him or her teach a how-to. Show your retail products in action, and offer discounts on products used. See if your vendor/product salesperson can donate freebies and signage for the event. Throw in some food and giveaways. And, of course, take lots of pictures and post them online.

No matter what the event, publicize it heavily. Send word to the papers, and promote via social media and flyers, etc.

Get Out!
You don't have to have these seminars in your place of business. You could also take them elsewhere, reaching another base of potential customers. Think businesses, colleges, even retirement villages.

TIP 117

Artistic Director Contest

Hold a competition between your stylists in a busy public place like a mall. Get the public involved by letting them judge the results. Give each stylist a set time to prepare a model. Then, put the stylist's name on the back of the salon T-shirts the models are wearing. Have spectators and passersby vote for their favorite results, and include a place on the voting slip for them to list their email. The winning stylist gets the title of "Artistic Director." Make sure everyone casting a vote gets a business card or coupon to the salon with the name of the stylist they voted for. This is also a great event to do at a fashion show, no matter how large or elaborate.

See step-by-step instructions for implementing this idea in the **Implementation Guide** at the back of this book!

TIP 118

Celebrity Visit

If you know a celebrity, even a local celebrity, or know someone who knows one (think: Six Degrees of Kevin Bacon), try to get the celebrity in your salon. Film actors, sports figures, authors, politicians, and even well-known people in the beauty world—think stylists or makeup artists to the stars—are all good ideas.

Promote this event on all social media platforms and in traditional media like newspapers and radio (the radio may even want to broadcast at the event).

The day of the big event, take lots of pictures of your staff and clients with the celebrities. Having your salon known as *the celebrity hangout* will surely entice the celebrity chasers in your town to try out your salon.

TIP 119

Woo Back MIA Clients: The Gifts and Flowers

How do you win back MIA (Missing In Action) customers?

Well, how do you win back a scorned lover? With gifts and flowers, right? In this case, call and reach out; offer them a free service or gift.

Have a team meeting and speak to your stylists to figure out what customers they haven't seen in a while. Compile a list from your database. You can email, use social media, or send a paper invitation with a discounted service and product package designed for them. Let them know they're missed and that you'd love to see them again.

Slow Nights and Days
If you already have nights that are bopping with clients, why worry about those? Get your money's worth. But if there are nights or days so quiet you can hear a pin drop, take some action and lure people in the doors, even if you have to use a few bells and whistles. These are great times to call back those MIA clients, get them in the chair, and show them what they're missing.

PART 3

Get Ahead of Your Competition

BE BUSINESS SAVVY

TIP 120

Good Business Practices Win and Maintain Clients

"If you don't drive your business, you will be driven out of business."
—B.C. Forbes

As a salon owner or independent stylist, it's important to remember you wear many hats. You cannot only be a stylist; you must be a good businessperson, too. Everyone is responsible for building his or her book of business.

Some suggestions for growing your customer book are just smart business sense.

Five Tips for Business Success

1. Provide amazing customer service.
2. Stay current with the beauty industry, knowing the latest trends, products, and services.
3. Be aware of what your competitors are offering and for how much.
4. Be aware of the latest technologies and media to reach your target clients and better serve the ones you have.
5. Be willing to try new ideas—new products and new services. Don't ever become stagnant. If the idea doesn't work, fail forward: learn from it and move on.

Business Savvy
Time and Money
Potential Investments

Time

- Time to attend business and industry workshop and events
- Time to research, purchase, and learn business software
- Time to personalize customer service
- Time to research competition
- Time to develop a salon logo for branding and promotional items
- Time to learn techniques, and promote new products and services

Money

- Fees for business and industry workshops and events
- Travel expenses
- Cost of business books and classes to build your knowledge
- Cost of hiring a business coach
- Cost of salon software to keep track of client information
- Cost of cards and related mailing expenses for customer mailings
- Cost of hiring a graphic designer or branding expert
- Cost of new promotional items
- Remodeling costs

TIP 121

Build Your Business Skills

Remember, you are responsible for building your clientele. Read business books, attend workshops—maybe even hire a business coach. Take advantage of free events and one-on-one coaching with small business development centers. Put tried-and-true business tips to work in your own salon/spa/barbershop. The quicker you realize your job is a creative *business*, the quicker you'll fill your chair.

A few folks we trust with the knowledge you need to create a successful business are:

PBA Education—Professional Beauty Association: www.probeauty.org

Summit Salon: www.summitsalon.com

Empowering You Consulting: www.empoweringyou.com

Strategies Publishing Group: www.strategies.com

TIP 122

Keep Your Employees Happy

If you're an owner, check the pulse of your business on a regular basis. Embrace a culture of positivity, open communication, and unity. In my book *Salon Business: How to Manage a Salon in Good Times and Bad*, I call this the "salon's heartbeat." You can build your salon's heartbeat by doing things like the following:

- Show your employees you care about them.
- Hold team meetings. Invite your team to write down questions and concerns anonymously. Have a box for this purpose. At the meeting, discuss these issues and questions. This maintains a healthy, happy workplace.
- Explain your vision for the business. Show them the greater vision—you want your employees to be inspired, to feel free to share their creativity, to be jumping out of bed in the morning to come to work because they are a part of something greater than just a paycheck.
- Promote education—of products, new styles, etc.
- Emphasize and take opportunities to educate on customer service and to show your employees the same respect through your treatment of them.

TIP 123

Capture Client Info

Collecting data on your customers will help you to personalize and maintain these relationships, and it will bring them into your chair more often. Just as we pay attention and work on relationships with those we love, we need to do the same for our customers. Thankfully, today's salon software makes it easy to input information and does a lot of the work for us—for an example, check out Meevo by Millennium S.I. beauty management software: www.meevo.com. Collect information such as email address, birthday, first day of service, appointment history, favorite salon services, and products purchased. Keeping track of this information with the help of salon software is an easy way to lure people back. You can even program some software to automatically send out a coupon for special occasions or when a customer hasn't been seen for a certain number of days. How about if your client hasn't been back to the store for 30 days? The program may generate an email coupon to say, "We haven't seen you in a while, so here is 20 percent off your next visit!"

TIP 124

Handwritten Notes

Well, in today's world of emails and social media, receiving a handwritten note (and not a bill) in the mail is unexpected and it makes an impact.

Send your customers a thank you card after their first visit and on salon anniversaries. Send paper birthday cards and other cards if you hear of a death or a birth in the family, if someone gets married or graduates, or for any other special or notable occasion. These personal gestures go far toward building long-term client relationships—reemphasizing the personal relationship between you and that precious client.

It's the Little Things
Little things make a difference. Don't forget to remind your receptionist to show appreciation to everyone leaving the salon by saying, "Thank you for coming" and "Have a great day."

TIP 125

Pay Attention to Your Competition

While we may offer kick-ass services, we still need to pay attention to our competition. What's that they say? Don't get lazy? This applies to relationships and business.

Social media is a great way to keep tabs on the local competition. You can look at their websites, Facebook pages, and Twitter feeds; also look at review sites like Yelp to see what customers are saying. If customers are dissatisfied, for example, with a competitor's lack of something, you could be the one to fill that need!

Remember, people always want to save a buck. So if there's a salon next door or down the road with a product that's a few dollars cheaper, customers will likely go there to buy the product. However, you can draw them into your doors by offering a greater selection of products, specials and coupons, and free gifts or samples with purchase.

Warning
While it's good to stay competitive, don't get lost down the rabbit hole of comparison. Focus on your strengths. Highlight what makes you and your business special.

TIP 126

Merchandising

Develop a salon/spa/barbershop logo or hire a graphic designer or branding expert to design one, and start giving and selling promotional items to customers. All of these items must include your location and basic contact information. Ideas include T-shirts, hats, water bottles, coffee mugs, pens, keychains, sticky pads, and anything else your clients will use on a daily basis. Offer larger merchandise for sale to customers, such as baseball hats, coffee mugs, and water bottles; keep some for raffles and giveaways. By getting your business's name and logo out into the general public, you are significantly increasing your exposure to new customers.

Stickers
Put a sticker with your salon/spa/barbershop information on all bottles of retail styling products so anyone else—family member, roommate, friend—who uses the product will see the sticker and know where to purchase it.

TIP 127

New Product Offerings

Stay fresh and current. Keep things exciting. Don't let things grow stale. This works in business just as it does in relationships. Offering a new line of products can also draw new people into your salon.

And roll out the new product line in style. Promote it heavily via social media, big signage outside the salon, word of mouth, et cetera. Have a product-launch event with how-to sessions, wine, and appetizers.

Talk to your product salesperson to see if you can get free signage and samples.

TIP 128

Add Another Service

Learn how to do other things. Mastering several services creates more opportunity for you in the salon or barbershop. It's great to be a hair-color specialist (where most of the money is), but if you're a wizard at eyebrow threading or scalp massage, maybe if you're and expert when it comes to curls or elaborate braids.

Consider adding one of three kinds of services:
- Easy ones
- Popular ones
- Hot and new ones

Potential Add-Ons

- Eyebrow waxing
- Facials, steam treatments, deep-pore cleansing
- Falsies: eyelash application
- Hair extensions
- Head and neck massage
- Brainstorm some more. If you're a stylist, discuss with the salon owner. If you're a salon owner, brainstorm and decide with your team.

Tell each and every customer about these new services. Say something like, "Today I'm offering something new. It's only $20. Will you try it?" And, of course, promote the new services via social media, promotions, and events. For example, if you added waxing to your menu, how about scheduling Waxing Wednesdays and offering a discount?

Be Different
Consider adding a service the rest of the local salons don't have—some hot, new styling service like permanent makeup, eyelash growth treatments, etc.

Blowouts

Blowouts are a hot service taking the salon industry by storm. Many businesses catering just to blowouts, such as Drybar, are popping up around the country. In fact, single-service salons are a growing trend. Think of advertising—PERFECT DATE-NIGHT SERVICE! Twenty minutes and you're in and out. *The Daily Beast* did a great article on blow-dry bars and their popularity: "The true "tipping point" for Drybar was when women who have never had the luxury of a fabulous blowout gave in and started coming to the salon— realizing it is affordable, fun, and that they can't do their own hair even a margin as well as the stylists. It was a "mousetrap," he said, for the women who were already getting blowouts daily because of the speed and environment." [1] And they reach a large range of clients: "Blow-dry bars offer a product—an experience, rather—that brings housewives, CEOs, and 10-year-olds to a place they can relax, chat, and come out feeling like a new person—all for about $40." [2]

TIP 129

Make Your Salon Male-Friendly

Ten Ways to Make Your Salon More Man-Friendly

These tips are also great for barbershops that aren't already doing these things.

1. Be on time. Most guys don't like to wait.
2. Create a separate service menu for men.
3. Add a product line for men.
4. Make sure to include images of men in your promotional materials.
5. Make a section of your salon the grooming lounge.
6. Avoid overly flowery décor. Go modern, and think neutrals. This works for both men and women.
7. Choose scents that appeal to both genders; this includes soap in the restroom.
8. Include guy-themed magazines in the waiting area (sports, current events, business).
9. If there's a big game, put it on the TV in the waiting room.
10. Have some guy-themed events: father/son nights, cops and firemen nights, craft beer night, etc.

TIP 130

Become a Makeup Specialist

Become a makeup specialist. The word will get around town quickly that you offer this service. Target brides especially when starting out. Attend some bridal shows; partner with a bridal shop or wedding planner.

Professional makeup application is not just for brides, however. Consider these ideas:

- Offer quick, flawless makeup application for every day: the everyday makeup package. Customers can pop in for a quick visit before or after work for the happy-hour package. This gives them the ability to feel like they are the most beautiful woman in the room every day and at any time.

- All women have important events to attend or dates to impress. Offer some date-night or big-night promos.

- Consider being a cover-up specialist. Sunspots, age spots, dark spots—it doesn't matter what you call them—most of us have them. Offer and promote this service as well. Sell a line of cover-up products.

Being a diversified salon will guarantee new clients not only looking for the newest style or hair color. Makeup doesn't take up much room in the salon, and the buy-in for your initial setup is not that expensive.

TIP 131

Make More Money from Your Current Clients: Suggest Additional or New Services

Just Ask
While you have the client in the chair, suggest an add-on. They're in the mood for beauty, they're right there, and if you tell them they need it, they're going to listen.

Just as we get comfy in our relationships and fall into the "let's stay in and watch movies and order a pizza" rut, we fall into a routine with our clients. Break out of the routine. Suggest new services to them. Try to personalize the suggestions to things you know they'll like. Start small if they're budget-conscious. Suggest a date-night blowout. Maybe eyelash extensions. Or you should come in for a makeover before your next date.

If there's a product or service you're just absolutely in love with, share it. People can sense the difference between someone just trying to sell them something and someone who is honestly excited. Salesmanship should come from believing in the product or service being sold.

Get your client in your chair more than every 6 weeks by simply suggesting additional services.

Set Goals and Track Success
To track success, set weekly goals of how many people you will suggest an additional service or product to, and keep a checklist of successful follow-ups to your suggestions. You'll soon see there's power in THE ASK.

TIP 132

Brand Your Recipes

Have signature menu items for your services. Every salon, for example, has a cut and color, but give your salon services special names. Be different; make it fun. Create your salon/spa/barbershop's *recipe menu*. This will set you apart from your competition. Your recipes are the pride of your business. Brand them outside of your salon/spa/barbershop to reach a new market.

Fun Service Names

Remember, get creative and get fun, but stick with your salon's vibe.

The Pedi-Cure: a luxury pedi with aromatherapy

Drop Dead Red: your signature red color formula

Summer Love: highlights and tints for that perfect pre-summer color

Unbelievable Updo: your most architectural or adventurous updo

And menu items like:

Chocoholics Beware

The Post-Breakup Menu

Sacred Desert

Dare to Try

Love is Near

Who Said You Can't?

TIP 133

Location-Specific Services: Cater to Your Location and Its Clientele

Get creative, and think of the services your location needs. Clients in snowboarding/skiing towns may need moisturizing treatments to protect skin (faces and hands) and hair sealants/protectants. Those on the coast who spend a lot of time in the water could use deep-conditioning products to prevent their hair from getting dry and brittle. You could even create a separate, fun menu for location-specific services.

TIP 134

Be the First in Town to Offer a Hot New Treatment or Technique

As a beauty-industry professional, you need to keep up with the latest trends and services. Attending industry trade shows and events keeps you on the up and up. So does paying attention to popular culture—popular magazines and blogs.

Check out your competition, and offer a hot, new service your competitor doesn't have. Promote heavily via social media. You could even launch the new service with a fun event.

TIP 135

Offer Memberships for Guaranteed Income

Memberships are a smart way to collect revenue that is dependable and guaranteed. If you charge an annual fee of, say, $45 and you sign up 1,000 clients, that's an extra $45,000 of guaranteed income with no extra overhead. Take a look at Massage Envy, for example. If you join its monthly membership program, you receive one free massage each month and discounts on other services. Salons could include products or product discounts in its packages as well. Also consider levels of membership: Bronze, Silver, and Gold, for example, with different services and price points.

Promote these membership packages like crazy via social media and word of mouth.

Website Ordering
List these membership packages on your website, and have a way for clients to purchase them on their own. Instant sales.

What should you include in your membership? Here's a list of possible services, specials and treatments, but rely on what you know about your clients to design the best program possible.

- Priority Booking (reserve a few spots every day for your priority members)
- Free services with every treatment (include the blow-out with every cut)
- Gift bags full of product samples (get these from your distributors)
- Member Appreciation coupons, events, discounts, and freebies

TIP 136

Gifts with Purchase and Samples

Gifts with purchase draw people. Why do you think the makeup counters put on these promotions each season? How many times have you gone to buy your makeup or planned to do so when the counter was having a gift-with-purchase promotion? Well, why wouldn't this work at your salon/spa/barbershop? These gifts with purchase could be a nice gift bag full of product samples (that you may be able to get for free from your product vendors). Make the bag and packaging pretty so that clients see the value. Just as makeup counters do, put a display on the counter with the gift bag and samples laid out to draw attention to the promotion. And advertise, advertise.

Tote Bags
Package free gifts in an inexpensive tote bag with the salon logo on it. Instant advertising as your customer carries it all over town.

Samples can lead to future sales of the full-price product. Ask your vendor for coupons to go along with the sample as these will also draw customers back into the salon.

TIP 137

Retail Boutique

If you have the space and you're not selling retail, start today. Create a space for shoppers, not only salon clients. Stock it with products that cater to the people in your demographic. Your salon will become a beauty retail boutique. This brings in the curious shopper looking for the newest hair products. Having a retail boutique is especially important if you are located in an area that gets foot traffic. Once a person walks into your salon/boutique, it's up to you and your staff to convert him or her to a salon client.

TIP 138

Salon or Barbershop Décor

Add a Barber's Pole, Get More Business
Everyone knows what a barber's pole stands for. It's an international symbol. So for all you salons and spas that do men's hair, ADD ONE! It's a cheap investment.

Sometimes, it's the salon/spa/barbershop itself that needs to be revamped. If your salon is stuck in the 80s, for example, with Home Interiors pictures and fake flowers caked with dust, who is going to want to go there? And if they do walk in, they may just walk out, making some kind of excuse about an emergency call. (By the way, this is a great tactic to end a horrible first date. But that's for another book.) Who wants to walk out smelling like Aqua Net and looking like she just came off the set of *Dallas*? (Yes, another 80s show.)

If your shop has had the same outdated look for years, perhaps it's time for an upgrade. Use well-lit display cases to showcase your retail, and use bright colors and accents to make your salon pop. People associate the look of your salon with the work you do. Fact is, when you remodel, you can increase your total sales over 20 percent in the first year from the change.

Even simple changes like a fresh coat of paint or fresh pictures on the wall can make a difference.

Keep in Mind
Remember to factor in how a remodel could disrupt business. Will you have to close for a while? If work can occur while customers are there, would it disrupt their view of the salon's environment? Consider whether the overall benefits are worth any costs.

Shameless Plug
We have some great books out on the subject of salon and barbershop remodels.

- *The Salon Building Bible*
- *Ready, Set, Go! The Start-Up Guide for Opening, Remodeling, and Running a Successful Beauty Salon*
- *Ready, Set, Go! The Start-Up Guide for Opening, Remodeling, & Running a Successful Barbershop*

Do YOU Need a Makeover?
Remember, you are a walking billboard for the beauty industry, and if YOU look like you're behind the times—tacky makeup and outdated hairstyle, for example—then people aren't going to trust you to make them look fresh and current. But you already know this.

TIP 139

Get Out of the Salon

If you want to see the newest trends and offer these beauty secrets to your clients, getting out of the salon is a must. Attend beauty trade shows and business seminars to get fresh ideas, network with others (including vendors), and learn new beauty techniques and business tips to bring back to the salon.

Staying fresh and current is key to attracting new customers. And the sooner you view what you do as not only creative but also a creative *business*, the quicker you'll begin to fill that book of business and see your profits increase.

OUT-OF-THE-BOX IDEAS

TIP 140

Think Outside the Box

Sometimes, dating outside your type can land you the love of your life. In the case of business, trying a new thing or reaching out to a new client group can yield a greater book of business.

Some ideas for generating interest in your business and gaining new customers are a little quirky. These might make you laugh or groan, but either way, they'll grab your attention—and that of your potential clients. If you have an idea of a way to generate business that's fun and funky, even a little wacky, go ahead and give it a try (especially if it's an idea that isn't high in cost or time). As long as it isn't something that will hurt your reputation or your existing clientele, anything you try could be the attention-grabber that wins you clients.

Less Competition
The thing about thinking outside the box is you'll have very little competition in that market because no one's thought of the idea. Finding neglected spaces in niche markets and filling them can be golden and lead to long-term clients—just as dating "outside your type" can lead to the love of your life.

Coming up with these out-of-the-box ideas is a fun way to build morale. Have a staff contest for the best idea, and reward the winner with a gift certificate to a local restaurant or theater.

Out-of-the-Box Ideas
Time and Money
Potential Investments

Time

- Time to make a list of out-of-the-box ideas and people and places to reach out to (or to have an employee contest to come up with ideas)
- Time to reach out to them
- Time to attend or participate in events
- Time to volunteer in reputation- or name-building activities

Money

- Donuts and/or coffee
- Marketing costs
- Cost of discounted or free services
- Related costs for planning an event or promotion

TIP 141

Be Your Town's Beauty Expert

A great way to get new customers is to be known as a local expert on all things hair or all things beauty. You can do this by volunteering at a local radio station or publication to be its "Beauty Consultant." Host a weekly radio show where you give beauty tips and the latest styling advice. Similarly, you can write a beauty column for a local newspaper or magazine. The public associates people they hear on the radio or read in the paper with expertise, and everyone wants their hair done by the local expert.

TIP 142

Colleges and Universities

If you live in a college or university town, have you considered how your services could benefit students?

Freshmen and Transfer Students

Think of college students as new residents. They're basically moving into a new neighborhood for two to four years. They're missing their moms and dads, their family. Be their home away from home.

Send a targeted mailing with a salon menu and coupons to freshmen and transfer students. Get a booth and get involved in some of the freshmen fairs (talk to the folks in the Student Affairs office). Drop off salon menus and coupons to the residence hall directors. Put up flyers around campus with tear-off coupons.

Student Affairs Office

Visit the Student Affairs office to see how you can get involved. This is the office involved in creating campus events and entertainment; it's also involved with the residence halls and sororities and fraternities.

Sororities and Fraternities

Think about sororities and fraternities and all the formals and themed parties they have. They want to look good! Become the go-to salon or barbershop for all their events.

Start by finding out the fraternity and sorority liaisons. Sometimes, these are faculty sponsors or persons hired particularly for this purpose. Find these persons through the Student Affairs office on campus. Ask if they can give sorority or fraternity members some brochures and coupons.

Partner with College Career Services

Partner with Career Services at the local college. Why? Because these organizations put on career-etiquette talks and fashion shows. Why not be the featured salon/spa/barbershop? Show participants how to style their hair and do their makeup with elegance and class. This is a great way to get the word out about your salon and highlight some of your retail products. And once students get ready for their job interviews, they'll think of you. Even college staff may show up for an appointment.

Fashion-Show Fun

If you're partnered with a local clothing boutique, why not plan a job-interview fashion show along with the Career Services office?

Freebies and Promotional Items

Talk to your product suppliers and see if they can provide you with product samples. Also give out your business card along with a promotional item(s) containing your salon/spa/barbershop's name, logo, and website.

Other Ideas

- Put an ad with a coupon in the college newspaper, especially the first few issues of the year.
- Post flyers all around campus (bookstore, student union, residence halls, bathroom stalls).

TIP 143

Visit Construction Sites: Chase Down the Men

If the construction site is for a new apartment building, consider all those potential new customers. Get the inside scoop from the workers on when the development will be finished. Also talk to the apartment manager, and make sure your salon menu and some coupons get into the mailboxes of the new residents or in the new-resident welcome package.

TIP 144

Reach Out to Accountants During Tax Season

Your accountant knows people and he certainly knows where you stand financially, so ask him if he could pass out a few cards or give you a few referrals. It's worth a shot and he may feel obligated since you're a client.

TIP 145

Dogwalk Fashion Show

We have all seen or at least heard of the catwalk, or fashion-show runway, for the biggest clothing manufacturers in the world. Well, why not have your own "Dogwalk"—or fashion show for your clients' dogs? In 2013, rescue dogs trotted the runway to present Ralph Lauren's Fall accessories collection. There's no reason your salon can't have the same type of doggie fashion show. Invite the whole town, make it fun, and spread the word through your local radio stations and clients. Everybody loves their pets. Make this a family night. Have your stylists help groom and dress the dogs up for the runway. What a great way to spread the pet love in your town. The local news may even send a crew over to film the event. This is a great way to get free exposure for your salon/spa/barbershop.

And yes, CAT LOVERS, you can do a catwalk too.

TIP 146

Parties

What a great idea to draw in new clients. You can host birthday parties, Sweet 16s, girls' night out, and bachelorette parties. These and other social events can be held after hours or during specially reserved times. Have some of your new employees work the event to gain new customers. You can also bring your skills *to* a party. Remember slumber parties? Now how cool would it be to have a real makeup artist or stylist do up everyone's hair and makeup and teach some beauty tips? Leave some salon menus and coupons with the girls and their parents.

Girl Scouts
What about reaching out to **Girl Scout** troops? They're always looking for field trip and activity ideas. Think, too, of the troop leaders and the parents—all potential customers! You could even sponsor the troop or one of its events. And everybody buys Girl Scout cookies, so let troop members camp out and sell them in front of the salon. What a great way to get new walk-ins. And how many of your customers have kids who are Girl Scouts? Let them take turns selling their cookies outside.

TIP 147

Halloween and Costume Services

Why not be the salon that offers spooky makeup for Halloween? If you have a stylist with experience in theatrical/movie makeup, use this as a selling point. If there's an anime or other costume conference or event coming to town (steampunk, Star Trek, etc.), heavily promote this service to that population. What a hit this type of makeup skill would be for parties, too. Take load of pics for social media.

TIP 148

Reenactment Groups

Reach out to local reenactment groups—medieval, Civil War, etc.—and offer to be their go-to stylist or barber. These groups are often having special events, and looking spectacular and having hair and makeup authentic to the period is very important. These groups are very close-knit and connect often with other districts that aren't necessarily far away. You could win a lot of new clients who also start coming to you for the "day-to-day" as well. Post lots of pictures of your creations. You could even sponsor group events.

PART 4

Giving Back

TIP 149

Give Back and Show Support

"For it is in giving that we receive."
—Francis of Assisi

The main goal of this book is to fill your chair or salon with clients. Wouldn't it be wonderful if while doing so, you're also helping others along the way? The old expression is that karma is not a coincidence. If you do good things, good things happen. So why not make this your destiny?

Read on for tons of ideas on how to find and get involved in causes and organizations near and dear to your heart—and your community's.

Community-Involvement Page
Designate a page of your website or Facebook to your community involvement. There you can list causes you support, post upcoming events, and provide pics from past events.

Give Back and Show Support
Time and Money
Potential Investments

Time

- Time to research organizations or events to volunteer with
- Time to reach out to organizations
- Time to volunteer and participate in charity events
- Time to plan and implement events in your salon/spa/barbershop that benefit charities

Money

- Discounts, promotions, and related event costs to celebrate service workers in the community
- Donuts and coffee
- Business cards
- Marketing materials and print costs
- Charity donations (money, products, services)

TIP 150

Choose Your Charity

Come together at a staff meeting and vote on a charity to support. When choosing a charity, consider the following:

- What causes and organizations are important to you and your staff?
- Are there community events that excite you and your staff?
- What causes are near and dear to your customers' hearts? Are there events that your customers would be interested in?
- What organizations could benefit from your services and donated products?

Personal passion for a cause is contagious. It will rub off on you and those around you. And choosing a particular charity to focus your attention on and then building a long-term relationship with it will also build your reputation as being a place of business that truly cares about others.

Commitment-Phobic or Too Busy?
If promoting or getting involved with a charity as a salon owner or stylist seems too overwhelming due to time restraints or family obligations, get involved with a charity such as Toys for Tots (**www.toysfortots.org**). One of its major components is simply putting a large box in the salon you own or work in for people to deposit gifts.

TIP 151

Join a Local Volunteer Organization

Volunteer your time to those in need. By becoming part of a local organization, you are not only making a difference but also building relationships and developing contacts. Don't be afraid to tell people what you do for a living.

TIP 152

Host a Fundraiser

Offer your volunteer organization or your clients your place of business to host a fundraising activity. You'll get new people into your building (potential customers!) and perhaps even some positive press out of it. Schedule the event on a slow day or a day that you are normally closed. Make sure you have staff on hand to meet and greet.

TIP 153

Customer Appreciation Days

It seems pretty obvious, but just as you need to work on your romantic relationships, we also need to continually show our customers how much we appreciate them. Have special customer appreciation days throughout the year with discounts, freebies, snacks, and drinks laid out throughout the day. Promote via social media, flyers, and word of mouth.

> Be sure to pamper those VIPs with discounts, gift bags, and special events. Whatever you do to make your ordinary clients feel special, you should go above and beyond for your VIP clients.

TIP 154

Think Pink: Breast Cancer Awareness

October is Breast Cancer Awareness Month. Have your salon team wear pink or a pink accessory for the entire month, and give customers a discount if they wear pink as well. Support the month by creating charitable events, and alert your local media. You could also sponsor local events supporting the cause.

Create a pink shopping area, giving a percentage of the sales to a breast cancer foundation of your choice. Decorate the entire salon with pink ribbons, pink up your salon's windows, and/or put fresh-cut pink flowers at your front desk. Many salons also offer pink hair extensions or feathers during October.

If you have customers who currently have cancer or who have survived cancer, pick a special day in the month and provide free services for them.

Fashion Show to Honor Survivors
What about putting together a fashion show with breast cancer survivors as the models? Pamper them—do their hair and makeup, give them a fabulous style. Make these women feel gorgeous and celebrated. See if you can partner with a local clothing store, and get the media involved.

TIP 155

Think Red: Heart Disease Awareness

Heart disease is the number-one cause of death in the United States and the number-one killer of women. So why not bring some awareness to the cause by participating in Heart Month or National Wear Red Day, held each February? This is a good cause for both salons and barbershops to support.

Just as breast cancer has its pink campaigns, heart disease has its red ones. So "red up" your salon/spa/barbershop for heart-health month. Have your stylists wear red or the National Wear Red Day red-dress pin to show support. Decorate your business with red flowers and other accessories. Offer specials on red manicures, red hair coloring, etc. Give discounts to those with red hair or who wear red when they come in for their appointments. You could even have a "red" fashion show in which you partner with a local clothing boutique and bring attention to the cause (and your businesses). Have survivors be the models if you can.

"Brother-and-Sister" Partnership Idea
A salon/spa and a barbershop might partner with each other and a local boutique for a fashion show celebrating heart disease survivors. Both guys and gals look snazzy in red. This event would not only bring attention to the cause but this brother-and-sister partnership would also promote goodwill among local, competitive businesses, drawing positive media attention.

If one of your customers has a family member with heart disease, consider raising money for the family (creating awareness for the cause is a side effect). Customers like to see a business support a cause, especially if it's close to home. You could even sponsor community events, bringing attention to the cause.

TIP 156

Monthly Causes

Almost every month has a major cause attached to it, so think about being the "give-back" salon/spa/barbershop and planning something special each month. Or pick a cause dear to you and your stylists, and build some events and promotions around the cause during its special month.

Just a few examples:

February: Heart Awareness, Black History
October: Breast Cancer, Domestic Violence Awareness
November: Diabetes

Put "health awareness months, weeks, and days" into your search engine to brainstorm more ideas.

TIP 157

Shelters and Recovery Programs

Domestic Violence and Women's Shelters

Women in shelters are hurting in many ways, and not only that, but many have to start over from scratch. This includes finding work. Your salon could be a blessing to these women. Simply receiving a new haircut, manicure, or style could give them a boost of confidence. And showing these women how to style their hair and do their makeup will help them feel better prepared as they get out there and apply for jobs. You could host an event or volunteer once a month, setting up a station and giving haircuts, hairstyles, makeovers, or manicures—whatever your specialty.

Men's Shelters and Recovery Programs

Life on the street or battling addiction takes it toll on the appearance. Unkempt hair, messy facial hair, dirty fingernails—all these things make it hard for these men to get back on track to a solid life: a job, financial security, a home. Consider having a barbershop/male grooming night. Enlist some of your barbers or stylists. Have a shaving/beard-trimming area, haircut chair, or even a nail-trimming area.

TIP 158

Give-Back Day

If a cause is near and dear to your heart, hold a give-back day in which a portion of the day's proceeds goes to the charity. You could create an event around the give-back day and promote it via traditional and social media. If a client or a client's family member is struggling with a major health issue or burden (house fire, cancer, etc.), you could personalize the event toward helping that person.

TIP 159

Be Welcoming to the LGBT—Lesbian/Gay/Bisexual/Transgender Community

Gay, lesbian, bisexual, and transgender people want to know they have a place where they feel accepted and comfortable with those around them. So be pro-LGBT. Why not be ahead of the curve and make your salon or barbershop the go-to place for all genders in your community? Let your customers know that LGBT are welcome. Word will spread through your town, and you will quickly have a beautiful, more diverse clientele.

The Simplest Gestures Go a Long Way
Including a small rainbow on your door and front-desk area and on your website is a subtle yet appreciated way for LGBT to know they are welcome.

TIP 160

Student and Teacher Appreciation

Student Day

Support your local university or community college by starting a Student Day each week in which students show their ID and get a discount. Post a sign in your salon/spa/barbershop and on campus bulletin boards advertising this special day for students. Students are often on a tight budget, but they also care about looking their best. By offering a special day each week they can come in for a discounted service (maybe an otherwise slow day), you'll be sure to have a full house and can start developing long-term relationships.

Teacher Appreciation

Similarly, have a teacher appreciation day with discounts, freebies, and drinks and snacks. Celebrate these individuals who work so hard for so little. Advertise the event in the media, and craft a letter to send to all the local schools. Take lots of pictures.

TIP 161

Event Donations

Join a board of directors or participate in a fundraising event by donating products and free services from your salon for a raffle or an auction. Your name will be seen and/or heard by participants, and the winners must redeem the prizes in person (and hopefully will become new customers after their service). Do as many of these as you can find in your community: school events, church auctions, charity events, and apartment-complex or homeowner-association community events. This is a great way to build your salon name and pick up new customers.

TIP 162

Sponsor a Local Charity Event or Community Organization, or Form a Team

Sponsoring a local charity event or community organization—think little league or Girl Scouts—is a great way to get your name out into the community in a positive way. When you sponsor something, your name is put on lots of promotional materials—flyers, T-shirts, etc. Or form a team for a charity event like Relay for Life or even a 5K (especially those for charitable causes). This will draw your salon family even closer together.

TIP 163

A Newsworthy Salon

There are times in your business that a heartwarming story develops in your salon/spa/barbershop. It may be children shaving their heads and donating their hair to cancer patients or helping a family in need. If something newsworthy is happening in your salon, send word to the papers and/or see if a radio station would want to broadcast live at the event. Take some pictures, and post on social media.

The key is to promote your salon and staff while giving back and helping people in need. Remember, too, that media attention is also drawing attention to the cause, so it's a win-win for all involved.

TIP 164

Locks of Love

Locks of Love (according to its website) is "a public non-profit organization that provides hairpieces to financially disadvantaged children in the United States and Canada under age 21 suffering from long-term medical hair loss from any diagnosis."[1]

How can your salon help? First, go to the Locks of Love website and download a registration packet to become a supporting salon: http://www.locksoflove.org/get-involved/. The kit includes all kinds of helpful materials, including press release templates and media ideas.

Have a sign in your salon's window and an icon on your salon's website saying something like "Proud Locks of Love Supporter."

You can even plan special events around the cause.

TIP 165

Pamper People Who Could Really Use It

Provide free services to populations and individuals who could really use a boost.

Think makeovers, beauty treatments, facials, massages, fashion shows.

Make a visit to some of the following places. This may take some planning; talk with the staff, set up a date, and spread the word.

Consider:

- Hospitals
- Cancer wards
- Shelters
- Nursing homes
- Individual clients who are struggling with something (In this case, you might send a card with a certificate inside for a free service.)

IMPLEMENTATION GUIDE

Now you have lots of ideas for generating new clients and improving customer retention. So how should you go about implementing an idea? Some of the ideas are pretty basic and don't take a lot of business planning, but other ideas are more involved. In this section, we provide a step-by-step example to implementing an idea, discussing some of the aspects you may have to consider when launching a new program. For this example, we'll use *116. Artistic Director Contest*. You may want to reread the tip to refresh your memory.

1. Determine Your Budget

You'll have to decide what it's going to cost to implement any idea. In this case, the cost is supplies needed to do the contest. You'll need:

- Microphone and speaker (you can rent one from a party store). **Estimated cost (for rental):** $100.

- T-shirts printed with your salon's logo, address, and telephone number on the front. (Make sure they look nice enough to wear after the event.) You will need twice as many T-shirts as you have members on your team. **Estimated cost:** $15/shirt x 16 shirts = $240.

- Voting cards made with a space to vote but also spaces to fill in the name, address, phone, and email of the person voting. You can create these yourself and print or have copies made (put two on a page). **Estimated cost:** $0.50/page x 50 pages (100 cards) = $25.

- You will also need salon appointment cards, and each of your staff should have business cards to hand out (personal or salon-generic). **Estimated cost:** Nothing; you should already have these.

- Promotional items and product samples with your salon's logo, address, and telephone number imprinted or stickered on them. **Estimated cost:** Talk to your vendors/product salespeople! Very often, you can get these items for free.

- You'll give out a free service, such as a makeover, to interest people and entice them to vote. **Estimated cost:** Time and product, no dollars.
- **Total estimated cost:** $415.
- **Total budget (add 20 percent contingency since this is just an estimate):** $488.
- Keep in mind you may need to pay a facility rental fee depending on where you hold your event. This cost could vary wildly, from a couple of hundred to tens of thousands of dollars.

2. Schedule Your Event

Pick a date for your event. You'll need one full day when you can close your salon. The slowest day normally is Monday, so this may work out perfectly, especially if your salon is brand new.

You may need to have a couple of available days because you may need to coordinate with the venue where you're holding your event (see Step 3).

3. Pick Your Place

Wherever you decide to hold your event, there needs to be lots of people passing by. Unless your salon is located inside a busy mall, you will not be able to just do this outside of your salon. Consider these options:

- Main street or other high-trafficked street
- Outside a local supermarket
- Shopping mall
- Starbucks
- Municipal building
- Local gym
- Busy restaurant

- Victoria's Secret
- Bakery

Talk to someone at the business or facility to make sure it's okay with them that you're holding the event inside or outside their facility. Let them know you should generate extra business for the both of you. Win-win! Offer them some coupons or complimentary services.

Depending on where you are going to hold your event you may need to rent the space. In this case, bear in mind the cost can vary wildly, from the hundreds of dollars to the tens of thousands of dollars. You may also need to secure permits if you're holding an event in a public place or obtain special permits to serve alcohol. Always adhere to your local rules and regulations.

4. Line Up Models

You'll need one model for each stylist in your team. It could be a friend or family member or a new or VIP customer.

5. Spread the Word

To generate extra attention for your event, advertise. This can be with posted flyers at your salon, the place of the event, nearby businesses, etc. Talk it up on all your social media platforms. Make sure your stylists tell their customers to come out and support them and bring their friends. You might even get some coverage from a local paper or TV or radio station if you call and let them know about the event (maybe you combine this with a charity event, asking for a donation for each vote).

6. Event Day

   a. On the morning of the contest, each of your stylists will be given two-and-a-half hours to prepare his or her model. Stylists must produce the best, most fashionable, and most cutting edge yet commercial work they are capable of producing with their designated model.

If you have makeup artists, beauticians, nail technicians, etc., they should get involved as well, showing off their product.

The stylists are competing against each other for a salon promotion to the title of "Artistic Director," so it's important they put their heart and soul into their competition entry.

When the models are finished, each of them puts on a salon T-shirt along with the rest of the team. Pin a blank piece of A4-sized paper onto the back of each model's T-shirt, and write down in big letters the name of the stylist who created the look. Your stylists should also put on name badges!

b. When everyone's ready, leave the salon and head to the place you've picked for your competition. Once you arrive at the location, you need to organize your team. Line up your models so that everybody can see them. Give the stylists five minutes to fix any last-minute alterations. Then let the fun begin!

One of you needs to take charge of the microphone or megaphone while the rest of the team works the public. Your aim is simple: You ask people passing by to vote which stylist's model they like best. Once the voter has chosen, you ask the model to turn around to show the name of the stylist who did the work. Give the passersby a voting form and pen to fill in his or her nomination along with name and email address, etc. The voter then puts this nomination slip into the box for a chance to win a free makeover at your salon (or you could do a free haircut, style, etc.). Throughout your voting time period, use the microphone to keep reminding passersby you're giving away a free makeover. You can also hand out extra T-shirts or promotional items printed with your salon logo and/or sample products. Let your stylists get out there and talk to people. If members of the public ask what the winning stylist gets, let the stylist tell them. Make sure every passerby who votes for a model gets a salon appointment card with the name of the stylist he or she voted for.

c. At the end of the afternoon, with appropriate hoopla, state that the winner is about to be announced. First, draw the name of the winner of the free makeover. Have a certificate to hand to the winner. Then, announce the winning stylist and model. Make sure there are lots of cheers, including from the rest of your team.

7. Follow Up

There is an old saying in sales that says, "the fortune is in the follow-up." It's become an old saying for a good reason: it's true, and it works. It's true that following up with customers and clients new and old can be one of the most important business actions a business owner or self-employed person can take.

The follow-up can be as simple as sending out an email or card to each client telling them who won the contest and the free makeover. Also include a free blowout or consultation with the stylist they voted for. Make sure you contact the makeover winner directly if she wasn't there when the announcement was made.

8. Analyze

After implementing any idea, you want to analyze how it went. In this case, look at how many new names and addresses you have for your client database. If you picked a good place and time, you should have at least 100 new names. Keep up with how many of the coupons you passed out get used. Then, think about how many new clients you got compared to how much you spent. If you spent all your budget, will you get that back if you have six new clients? What about 12 clients? What about goodwill and return visits by your existing clients? After analyzing the contest and the results, decide whether this will be a repeat activity, maybe an annual event.

164 Ideas Implementation Checklist

◯ **List Needs**
Include any products you need to buy, contacts with phone and email you'll need, and content you have to create.

◯ **Plan Budget**
As discussed, costs include time and money. For this step, list money costs, but also be aware of how much time you'll spend implementing the idea.

◯ **Determine Schedule**
Pick the best time to execute your idea, considering your workload, other events or promotions, slow days, etc.

◯ **Execute**
Go for it! Buy that ad, create and hand out those coupons, exchange business cards with a partner.

◯ **Follow Up**
Follow up if necessary, such as sending thank you notes.

◯ **Analyze Results**
This might mean having a "How did you hear about us?" section on your new-customer card, counting saved referral cards or coupons, or just noting how often your customers talk about or thank you for a particular event or donation. Also get feedback from your salon team.

◯ **Repeat, or Try Again**
Based on your analysis, make this an ongoing promotion, schedule the event annually or monthly, or select another idea to try.

CONCLUSION

"We have to continually be jumping off cliffs and developing our wings on the way down."
— Kurt Vonnegut

Bottom line—did you get new clients?

These tips are easy to understand. Some may seem so commonsense you may have said, "OMG, really? How easy is *that*?" There is no rocket science here, no mathematical formulas, no graphs and charts. These principles are easy to understand and easy to apply.

And remember, not every tip will work the first time or be the best fit for your particular business. It's important to reflect on the success of any tip you try. Sometimes, something is worth another chance; we don't do everything perfect the first time. Think of the dating metaphor: How many first dates have you bombed? Or job interviews? But see if the tactic worked. What could make it better next time? What was successful? Did it bring in more clients? Cash flow? Did you break even? Did profits increase?

Sometimes, you will fail. No great effort was achieved without a few bumps and bruises. But fail forward.

Don't give up because you've had a few bad "dates." You will find the one eventually, and you'll figure out what works and what you want in the process. Be patient with yourself. In business, you will find the ones, the many, the cha-ching. if you keep learning and growing and putting yourself out there.

We have laid out the groundwork from the simplest ideas that cost nothing more than your time, with virtually no out-of-pocket expense, to those a bit more complex. One idea does not have to lead to another, but the success you have is based on one thing: your willingness to take the necessary steps and get going. Day in and day out.

JUST DO IT!

Nike's "Just Do It" tag line is said to be the best tag line of the 20th century. It cut across all barriers—gender, age, race, physical fitness level. Nike's goal was to make consumers believe they could be successful too. It allowed people to understand that if they set personal goals, these goals could be achieved to the point of greatness.

Ready, Set, Go! Books would like for you—the cosmetologist, barber, massage therapist, nail technician, or makeup artist—to follow the "Just Do It" tag line. We have one objective here for you: to become financially independent with more customers than you can handle. Read this book, take one or all of these ideas, and just do it. You read the book; now put it to use: **JUST DO IT!**

In order to turn these tips into new clients, you'll have to work hard—consistently and continually—to improve and ultimately reach your goals. Like a great athlete, success doesn't happen after one workout. It happens over time.

But we know your effort, persistence, and newfound "Just Do It" mentality will lead you to getting new clients and making more money. Cha-ching.

Do You Hear the Sound?
Jeff's Uncle Frank "The Mayor" Lignori

When I was younger, I would visit my uncle's barbershop in Staten Island, New York. Everything I remember about his shop screamed "neighborhood hangout"—both the older men and younger high school kids waiting in line to get their weekly haircuts. The place was humming with laughter, jokes, bantering, and just plain old nonsense. The kind of atmosphere you couldn't help but love. All the clients sharing stories and talking small-town stuff.

My uncle would not only give a haircut and shave but would, as he called it, "hold court." His clients would hang on to their seats just to see what the "mayor" would have to say. That was his nickname. He cherished that nickname long after he retired. His family and friends called him by that name only, and he loved it. My uncle was not only a good barber but also a good listener, salesperson, and mentor. His life was hair but his passion was business, and his goal was to cut every guy's hair in town no matter what age or race.

My uncle loved his business. Every time I would come in for a haircut, he would say to me, "Do you hear the sound?" I would say, "What sound?" Then he would whisper in my ear, "the sound of the cash register going 'cha-ching, cha-ching.'" His famous quote was "the register is ringing, and the coins are singing; the bills are rustling, so the mayor is hustling." I thought he was crazy, but he was just crazy in love with what he did.

He told me one day long after he retired that **the greatest part of coming to work was that he loved the sounds his barbershop made.** At 12, I had no idea what he meant, but later in life he explained to me, sharing his business success and what inspired him to keep his passion and desire to work hard, gain new clients, and retire at an early age with financial independence. He shared his philosophies with me. Here they are, simply stated:

- When the mayor was busy—and his shop was always busy—the sound of people laughing and talking sports, politics, and life in general gave him the motivation to work harder; it inspired him to make every customer happy and leave with a great haircut no matter how long he had to stand on his feet or stay open past closing. "This," he said, "was the **sound of success.**"
- "The register is ringing, and the coins are singing" was the sound of making money. Simply put, each time the cash register would open, the register would go cha-ching, cha-ching. His goal was always to make the cash register ring, again and again. This was the **sound of motivation.**
- Lots of different customers came in daily—old-timers, politicians, mailmen, fireman, police officers, and, of course, the local kids in the neighborhood. He told me this was the **sound of fulfillment.**
- Customers were his treasure chest. The more he had, the bigger the treasure. Each customer was to be treated as a king—one haircut at a time, one relationship at a time, one story at a time, and one day at a time. This was the **sound of wealth.**

The best part of this story was that every time he unlocked the door to his barbershop to start the day, it was like opening the door to a symphony. Jokingly, he called **the sound of making money the sound of music.** He said it made him feel good and motivated him to go in early, stay late, and come to work when he wasn't feeling well. Once he got behind his chair, all of life's problems would suddenly disappear.

My uncle, the mayor, closed the shop in 1988, but many of the things he did to gain new clients I shared with you in this book. Yes, they worked. The mayor attended sporting events and hosted cut-a-thons before they were called that. He did those for the Boys and Girls Club. He would cut every high school kid's hair for free during football, basketball, and baseball season. (Yes, loyalty was a must from the parents.) He made every local newspaper, doing so year after year. He sponsored sports teams, and each of the team's pictures adorned the walls of his barbershop. He was the president of the Italian American Club, joined the chamber of commerce, and was a deacon at Our Lady of Good Counsel Catholic Church. Does any of this sound familiar? Yes, these ideas are in the book—they do work, they worked then, and they will work now. Back then, there was no email, no fax, no texting, and no cell phones. If you wanted to connect with someone, you simply put out your hand. Yes, 50 years later these principles still apply.

In closing, the last thing my uncle said to me was, "Once you ring the register one time, you can ring it again and again and again but not without putting your hand out and saying hello with a big smile on your face." He then said, "How else would they know you're a barber in town?"

Frank "The Mayor" Lignori
Swifty's Barber Shop
1955–1988

Speed Dating with Celebrity Stylists

With speed dating, you're given three to five minutes to talk to people before you move to the next. Well, this is our version of speed dating. We reached out to celebrity stylists—people whose chairs are ALWAYS FILLED and who are known world over for their talents—and asked them a few basic questions, all a variation on these:

1. Do you feel you need a specific look to be successful in hair?
2. What's the best advice for getting new clients?
3. Do you have to be a salesperson even though you're a good hair person?

Consider this your chance to sit across from highly eligible stylists—well, ones whose talents and business are sought after world over. Read on and learn.

Chris Baran
Fuel Education Systems, President
Redken, Education Artistic Director
S.P.E.C. Artistic Director
"Put more AWE in your awesome."

1. Do you feel you need a specific look to be successful in hair?

Image is everything. Studies say that people will make an impression of you within the first 6 seconds of meeting. So, it's not rocket science to figure out that first impressions are what people remember. Celebrities pay thousands of dollars a year for personal hair, makeup, and wardrobe stylists to ensure that their first, second, and third impression is always great. Be nice wouldn't it—having your own troop to "put you together" every day. Why do I bring that example into play? Successful people know that success is directly proportionate to their look plus talent. It's no different for hairdressers.

Let me paint another picture for you. But first, change roles: you're the customer, and you walk into a salon. Two stylists are open. They both greet you. Both are enthusiastic, friendly, and truly interested in you. Too, unbeknownst to you, both are equally talented (a clever ploy to take out the talent issue and resolve the old joke that you always go to the hairdresser with the bad haircut because they did the good one).

Stylist A's hair color and style is on point, nails manicured, makeup is trendy but not over the top (obviously, if the stylist is male, the makeup would be a fresh face with groomed facial hair), clothes are fashionable and on trend. In other words, Stylist A is well put together.

Stylist B, while equally exuberant, has hair and makeup that is obviously a decade old—even you as a client recognize that. The clothes are from the same era, disheveled with bleach marks—still recognizable even beyond the black marker cover-up.

Simple question—WHICH ONE WOULD YOU CHOOSE?

2. What's the best advice for getting new clients?

The obvious answer—*word of mouth*. Let your work speak for itself, and have other clients recommend you. Like I said, obvious, but not always the most productive if you're building a new clientele.

What's the best way? One simple version—promote. The long version—"promote" is a fancy-pants word meaning "sell." Confidence sells. People are drawn to those who look like they know what they are talking about. Whenever you're around new people, tell them you're a hairdresser. And you know the first thing that they'll say is, "What would you do with my hair?" Voila!—an opening for an impromptu consultation. Remember, the one who asks the questions controls the conversation.

EXPERIENCE SELLS. Have you heard this one: *Fake it 'til you make it?* My humble opinion—that is El Toro Caca. Excuses aside, if you've done a technique, haircut, color, or up-style successfully more than two or three times, YOU'RE EXPERIENCED. Let people know. Show your Brag-umility. Say what? Brag with humility. Keep the focus on them and what you can do for them as opposed to how great you are—Brag-umility. People are turned off by people who are full of themselves and live on an I-land—*I, I, I, me, me, me*. However, selling yourself is nothing more than displaying a confidence in your own ability to improve someone's look with your hairdressing ability. People who are confident and assured with their own ability draw clients to them.

3. Do you have to be a salesperson even though you're a good hair person?

I want to debunk an old myth that has worked its grubby claws into our industry. But before, here's my disclaimer. I am creative, I love doing hair, and I AM A CAPITALIST. I love making money. There. I said it! Some people say, "Money can't buy happiness"— obviously a statement from those who don't have money. I've had none, and I've had lots—I like lots better. Nonetheless, I would sooner be crying in a Porsche than laughing on a bicycle.

People, you don't have to be creative, love what you do, and be poor. This industry offers so much potential for both (creativity and wealth). Where else can you raise your paycheck by suggesting a service or product the client wants and is happy to pay for—and the money goes to you? No-brainer.

Ok, here's the old myth—*I'm an artist, not a salesperson. I shouldn't have to sell.*

Let's play a quick game of word association. If you haven't played this game before, it goes like this. I say a word, and you immediately shout out the first word that comes to your mind. For instance, if I say, "house," you might yell out, "home," "cat," "dog," or so on. Got it?

So here's the word: "SALESMAN." Obviously, I can't hear your response, but when I ask this in a classroom, here are the responses I get: "liar," "selling me something I don't need or want," "greasy," "slick," "dishonest," "rip-off artist," "con," and other negative connotations. That negative image is what has become brain-engrained when people hear the word "SELL."

Let me ask you this. Presently or at some time have you had a girlfriend, boyfriend, wife, husband, or life partner? Was there some selling that went on beforehand? How many of you have children, nieces, or nephews (particularly of the young variety)? Are they not the best salespeople? LIFE IS SALES. Sales is nothing more than finding out what people want and helping them get it. Great salespeople help others find a solution to their problem in an honest, ethical manner.

To prove the point, think of a problem that you have in your career or personal life. Take a minute, and think of one.

Question: If I could solve it for you, would you pay me to help you solve it? YES OR NO?

If you said yes, we just did a sale. If you said no, God bless you! You don't have any real problems. Someone will always pay to have their hair problems fixed. Do you want them to pay you—or someone else?

Do you have to be a salesperson? Absolutely! Listen up! SALES = INCOME.

Beth Minardi
Stylist to the Stars
Owner of Minardi Color Line, Beth Minardi Color Lighting
Beauty Educator and Motivational Speaker

(Celebrities Beth has styled include, to name a few, Brad Pitt, Uma Thurman, Cameron Diaz, Julianne Moore, Kirsten Dunst, Evan Rachel Wood, Edie Falco, Christie Brinkley, Matt Dillon, Faye Dunaway, Rene Russo, and Willem Dafoe. Wowza!)

Dressing for success is a very important part of our job. Look great and you will succeed—and be respected. Look poor, disheveled, and not in fashion, and your clients will see you as a servant rather than a professional service provider.

The best thing I ever did to gain new clients was to have my existing clients refer a friend to the salon. I told them they would receive 20 percent off their next cut or color, and their friend, when they came in for their first service, would receive a professional haircut and professional hair-care gift—at no charge. Works like a CHARM, every time.

Pat Parenty
President of L'Oréal Professional Product Division

Obtaining clients is part of the process of being a professional cosmetologist. L'Oréal believes in higher education, and for the stylist who continues to learn and hone their skills, the process of professional growth and financial success will enable them to achieve their goals. L'Oréal strategy is not complex. A cosmetologist who learns better will earn better and live a better life in a field they love.

L'Oréal is in the forefront of fashion and design trends; as a professional cosmetologist, you should look the part and play an important role in defining each and every one of your guest's lives—making and changing them to look and feel amazing every time they sit in your styling chair.

Michelle Buhr Steimann
Director of Facilities
Ginger Bay Salons and Spas

(Ginger Bay has won countless awards, including the prestigious status of being one of Salon Today's top 200 U.S. salons and spas—its twelfth year of being chosen. The salon has also been featured in newspapers and magazines like The New York Times and Inc.)

We have found at Ginger Bay that the best way to obtain new clients—hands down—is guest referral programs. I recommend an incentive that rewards the referring guest with a free service or service dollars in the salon or spa.

We also believe in branded collateral. If you visit with us, everything has the Ginger Bay logo down to the tissue box in the bathrooms. Wear it loud and proud.

When it comes to dress code or how you should look as a professional, we believe that people look to us as the next fashion trend. We open their eyes to how they are supposed to look in the world and what is happening in not only hair but also makeup and clothes trends. The visual is everything to the client. The entire staff at Ginger Bay absolutely looks the part and adheres to an all-black professional dress code. This enables our guests to readily differentiate our team from other guests. Our team incorporates color into the black dress code with accessories. Complete hairstyle and makeup are a very important part of our female employees.

Professional appearance always creates a lasting impression and shows our guests we care enough to look our very best every time they walk through the doors of our business.

Best practices for a new cosmetologist finding new clients? Talk the talk and walk the walk. Constantly tell people what you do. Friends and family and neighbors are the first people you need to get into the salon. Social media and Facebook voting pages prove to be quite beneficial due to the viral activity as well as boosting. Tweet, text, and keep putting your hand out to tell people what you do and where they can find you.

Brayden Pelletier
Global Master Redken Artist and Educator
Owner/Master Stylist of Just B. Hair Salon

(Brayden's work has appeared on the runways of Marc Jacobs, Dessel, NYC Fashion Week, and the 2014 VMAs.)

Getting new clients is not that hard. Do Great Hair, and new clients will follow.

Education is a must—get as much as you can, every time you can. Get out in the streets and spread the word. Post before-and-after pictures on social media. And hashtag the heck out of them. Keep up the pace, put your hand out, and tell people what you do. Never be embarrassed of what you do; remember, you change people's lives by how good you can make them look and feel.

Dress for success. Remember, you're an image consultant. Black is a must. Start there. Once you've learned style, then start to express yourself. Remember, a client's first impression is the most important! Classic wins over trendy nine out of ten times.

Interview with Wallace Barlow
(from "4 Easy Steps to Building Your Clientele," Behind the Chair[1])

Master Barber
Andis Global Educator
Brand Ambassador for Minerva Beauty
Artistic Director for MAG Shears

1. **Identify the potential clients on your route.** "I started thinking about where I would go every day," Barlow explains, "before and after work. And I wondered, 'How many potential clients did I encounter along the way?' Target people at your coffee shop, favorite restaurants and clubs, at your church, at your child's day-care center, at the grocery store. These are people you know and like, so you know they will be happy with your work. And remember," he adds, "ten potential clients can turn into thirty. You pass by an entire book of clients on your way to and from work!"

2. **Connect with passion.** As you identify these potential clients, connect with purpose, passion, and professionalism that will prove why you are different from every other hairdresser. "Be genuine and humble," Barlow advises. "Say, 'I'm a new stylist, I'm building my book, your hair is gorgeous, and I'd love to work with you!'" Also, he suggests, be open to every opportunity. If someone compliments you on your stylish shoes or glasses, for example, seize that chance to let them know what you do and invite them to your salon.

3. **Give them a good reason to try you out.** If your salon doesn't already have a "try-me" system in place, sit down with your owner or manager to discuss some options. Explain that you are serious about building your business and that you will use this opportunity to build your book. At his salon, Barlow gave new stylists two cards each month that were good for a free service. He advised the staffers to hand them out to attractive employees in nearby boutiques and restaurants (no freebies for mom or Aunt Janice!). "I told them that if they made these people look great, they each had the potential to send thirty more people their way," Barlow notes.

4. Showcase your work on the best "models." Nothing sells beautiful hair like a beautiful person, so start assembling a portfolio of your work, showcased by the very best models. "Bring a camera into work," suggests Barlow, "and set up a plain backdrop." When you complete a great-looking client, touch up her makeup and take her photo. "Make it fun," he suggests. "Treat her like a rock star." Load the images on a disc, print them out at home, and place the photos in a book that you can show to clients, and to prospective clients. Take it even further, and send the photos to hairstyle books and magazines. If they publish your work, it's another great selling point!

Before you hit the streets, it's important to lay the foundation for success. After all, the football team can't win with the playbook if they don't have the fundamental running, passing, and kicking skills in place. Barlow's "basics" include:

- **Dress for Success.** "If you want to be a rock star, look like a rock star," he says. "When I walk into a salon and spot the best-dressed stylist in the room, I'm already sold, even if that person isn't necessarily the best cutter."

- **Be on Time.** "Early is on time," declares Barlow. "On time is late."

- **Make Every Day an "A" Day.** Everyone has "A" days and "B" days, but when successful people are having a "B" day, they get back up and keep going. "Attitude is everything," says Barlow. "You have to wake up with it, come to work with it, and leave with it."

- **Have Faith in Yourself.** "Other people often told me how good I am, but because of my past I had trouble believing them," Barlow reveals. "But I learned that even if you're not where you want to be, you must have faith in your ability and faith in the people who believe in you."

- **Bring Your Passion.** "Be passionate or go home; it's as simple as that," says Barlow. "Anyone can be average and work three days a week, and that's fine. But if you really want to excel, you have to commit to this as a career. Live it and love it!"

"Connect with purpose, passion, and professionalism," says Barlow.

Larry Kane
Salon Co-Owner, Jonathan Kane Salon and Spa
Vice President of Sales for Coppola Beauty, LLC (Peter Coppola) Products

What is the best way to get new clients and walk-ins?

The best way to attract new guests is to do great work. It will speak for itself and pay huge dividends. Having a strong referral program helps as well. We use Millennium Software and their rewards program by rewarding clients with points for referrals, prebooking, and trying additional services. Backing those two components up with a good social media presence helps too. Being enfolded in the community is also really helpful. Support the kids, and the parents will come. We support local school districts with raffle items, ads in their school programs, and demos in their classes.

With regard to walk-ins, that is predicated on your location. As a freestanding building, we get few walks-ins; however, we get more than you would expect. If we were in a strip mall, I might opt for additional signage in the parking lot, sidewalk, or street side.

Is dress part of being successful as a stylist?

I have always thought that the better you look, the better the clientele you attract. Certainly the current way to dress in the salon varies from jeans and sleeveless shirts to all-out uniforms. You have to consider the general feel of the salon: urban, suburban, contemporary, cutting edge, etc. You can attract all of those and more as long as the focus is on customer service and not the staff. We employ a black-and-white dress code and a more relaxed dress code on Fridays.

Sam Villa
Founder, Chief Creative Officer, Sam Villa®
Global Educator for Redken
"Best Stylists 2015"
Favorite Platform Artist and Educator, Stylist Choice Award, 2007, 2011, 2012

1. What do you feel is the best way to get new clients?
It's all about self-promotion; the salon owner can do what they can, yet it's all about promoting yourself constantly outside the salon and behind the chair consistently. I am a firm believer that "people buy people, then they buy things." It's about connecting with people in today's world. A lot of times it's about the attitude—attitude is contagious, and sometimes as hairdressers behind the chair we need to ask ourselves whether ours is worth catching. Remember, it takes years to find today's client and seconds to lose them. Keep that in mind as a hairdresser behind the chair.

2. Do you feel that the way you look as a stylist helps you to get new clients?
I feel it's very important to look professional versus casual! First impressions are important, and unfortunately as human beings, we judge people on what we see on the outside versus what is inside. The outside has a voice as well as the inside. Both need to speak professionally. Imagine a great look with great communication skills, as communication skills build wealth, and the outside has a voice also.

Amy Carter
Director of Finances and Business Development
Empowering You Consulting
Salon Owner, Educator, Life Coach, and Salon Consultant

Dress for success:
I would say dress to the level of success you want to attract. We are in the

beauty industry; always have your A game on at work. Who are your ideal clients? Dress to their level.

Getting new clients in the door:

Referrals are key! I highly recommend driving business through your existing database.

Get clear on your ideal clients, and focus on them. Market to them, and design your business around their needs. So if you love soccer moms, then you need to open early so that they can be home by 2 p.m. Always speak hair and nails everywhere. Be proud of your work and what you do. You will be the *client attractor*.

APPENDIX

Dress For Success

[1] "What We Do," Dress for Success, accessed August 2, 2015, https://www.dressforsuccess.org/about-us/what-we-do/.

Dating (Client-Winning) 101

[1] Liane Beam, "Are You Stylish Or Trendy? Canadian Fashion Gurus Draw The Line," Faze, accessed July 31, 2015, http://faze.ca/are-you-stylish-or-trendy/.

Join and Attend Business Networking Groups and Events

[1] Ivan Misner, "Want to Join a Networking Group?" Entrepreneur.com, December 22, 2002, accessed July 31, 2015, http://www.entrepreneur.com/article/58210.

Trade Shows and Community Events

[1] Joseph Coupal, "More on How Trade Shows Can Boost Your Business - Newton, MA," *blog*, The Exhibit Source, June 29, 2013, accessed July 31, 2015, http://theexhibitsource.com/trade-show-exhibits-blog/tag/promotional_displays/.

[2] Ibid.

[3] Ken Krogue, "17 Skills for Highly Effective Tradeshow Events," Forbes.com, June 10, 2013, accessed July 31, 2015, http://www.forbes.com/sites/kenkrogue/2013/06/10/17-skills-for-highly-effective-tradeshow-events/.

Social Media

[1] Matt Petronzio, "U.S. Adults Spend 11 Hours per Day with Digital Media," Mashable, March 5, 2014, accessed July 31, 2015, http://mashable.com/2014/03/05/american-digital-media-hours/.

Create or Revamp Your Website

[1] Deluxe Blogmaster, "10 Internet Statistics to Inform Small Business Marketing Decisions," Deluxe, *Blog*, January 18, 2014, accessed July 31, 2015, https://ww.deluxe.com/blog/10-internet-statistics-inform-small-business-marketing-decisions/.

It's a MUST to Make Your Site Mobile-Friendly

[1] Victoria Woollaston, "How Often Do You Check Your Phone? The Average Person Does It 110 Times a DAY (and up to Every 6 Seconds in the Evening)," *Daily Mail*, October 8, 2013, accessed July 31, 2015, http://www.dailymail.co.uk/sciencetech/article-2449632/How-check-phone-The-average-person-does-110-times-DAY-6-seconds-evening.html.

Start a Beauty or Grooming Blog

[1] Swipely Team, "5 Brilliant Ideas for Hair and Beauty Salon Blogs," Swipely Blog, September 8, 2011, accessed July 30, 2015, https://www.swipely.com/blog/5-brilliant-ideas-for-hair-beauty-salon-blogs/.

Check-In Apps: Yelp Can Help

[1] Tory Johnson, "5 Free Ways to Attract New Customers to Your Small Business," ABC News (online), January 28, 2010, accessed July 31, 2015, http://abcnews.go.com/GMA/JobClub/tory-johnson-free-ways-attract-small-business-customers/story?id=8643027.

Television Ads

[1] Nancy Wagner, "How Much Does Television Advertising Really Cost?" *Houston Chronicle*, accessed July 31, 2015, http://smallbusiness.chron.com/much-television-advertising-really-cost-58718.html.

Radio Spots

[1] Brad Sugars, "Learn to Leverage the Radio," Entrepreneur.com, accessed July 31, 2015, http://www.entrepreneur.com/article/203246.

[2] IDEAGUY, "How Much Does Radio Advertising Cost?" Local Marketing Ideas, June 24, 2009, accessed July 31, 2015, http://localmarketingideas.com/how-much-does-radio-advertising-cost/.

Newspaper Ads

[1] Marc Prosser, "Newspaper Advertising Costs and More," Fit Small Business, December 5, 2014, accessed August 1, 2015, http://fitsmallbusiness.com/newspaper-advertising-costs/#.

[2] Ibid.

[3] "How Much Does a Local Newspaper Advertising Cost?" howmuchisit.org, accessed August 1, 2015, http://www.howmuchisit.org/local-newspaper-advert-cost/.

Coupon Mailings

[1] "Direct Mail Coupon," Valpak, accessed August 1, 2015, http://www.valpak.ca/advertise/products-services/direct-mail-coupons.jsp.

[2] Jaqueline Thomas, "Top 25 Places to Advertise Your Business Using Coupons," Fit Small Business, June 11, 2014, accessed August 1, 2015, http://fitsmallbusiness.com/coupon-advertising-ideas/.

[3] "Mailing Lists," Vistaprint, accessed August 1, 2015, http://www.vistaprint.com/mailing-lists.aspx?couponAutoload=1&GP=8%2f1%2f2015+1%3a24%3a40+AM&GPS=3575389446&GNF=0.

The Yellow Pages

[1] Kristina Knight, "Study: Yellow Pages Still Working for Many Consumers, Businesses," BizReport, March 19, 2014, accessed August 1, 2014, http://www.bizreport.com/2014/03/study-yellow-pages-still-working-for-many-consumers-business.html.

[2] John Tabita, "Google's Matt Cutts Recommends Yellow Pages," Haines Local Search, October 24, 2013, accessed August 1, 2014, http://www.haineslocalsearch.com/googles-matt-cutts-recommends-yellow-pages/.

Signage

[1] Jeff Grissler and Eric Ryant, "The Importance of Signage," in *Barbershop Now! How to Open a Barbershop* (Ready, Set, Go! Publishing, LLC, 2012).

Catch New Residents First

[1] "Mailing Lists," Vistaprint, accessed August 1, 2015, http://www.vistaprint.com/mailing-lists.aspx?couponAutoload=1&GP=8%2f1%2f2015+1%3a24%3a40+AM&GPS=3575389446&GNF=0.

Add Another Service

[1] Kelsey Meany, "Blow Dry Bars Are a Thriving Industry Disrupting the Salon Business," *The Daily Beast*, July 13, 2013, accessed August 1, 2015, http://www.thedailybeast.com/articles/2013/07/13/blow-dry-bars-are-a-thriving-industry-disrupting-the-salon-business.html.

[2] Ibid.

Locks of Love

[1] "What Is Locks of Love?" Locks of Love, accessed August 2, 2015, http://www.locksoflove.org.

Interview with Wallace Barlow

[1] "4 Easy Steps to Building Your Clientele," *Behind the Chair*, accessed August 1, 2015, http://www.behindthechair.com/displayarticle.aspx?ID=1423.